BROKE VEGAN ONE POT

OVER 100 SIMPLE PLANT-BASED RECIPES THAT DON'T COST THE EARTH

SAM DIXON

ASTER*

ASTER*

First published in Great Britain in 2022
by Aster,
an imprint of Octopus Publishing Group Ltd
Carmelite House
50 Victoria Embankment
London EC4Y 0DZ
www.octopusbooks.co.uk
www.octopusbooksusa.com

An Hachette UK Company
www.hachette.co.uk

Distributed in the US by
Hachette Book Group
1290 Avenue of the Americas
4th and 5th Floors
New York, NY 10104

Distributed in Canada by
Canadian Manda Group
664 Annette St.
Toronto, Ontario
Canada M6S 2C8

ISBN 978 1 78325 538 2

A CIP catalogue record for this book
is available from the British Library.

Printed and bound in Czechia

10 9 8 7 6 5 4 3 2 1

Senior Commissioning Editor:
Natalie Bradley
Editor: Sarah Kyle
Copy Editor: Jo Richardson
Art Director: Jaz Bahra
Designer: Rosamund Saunders
Photographer: Charlotte Nott-Macaire
Props Stylist: Anna Wilkins
Food Stylist: Sam Dixon
Assistant Production Manager: Emily Noto

Standard level spoon measurements are
used in all recipes.

1 tablespoon = one 15 ml (½ fl oz) spoon
1 teaspoon = one 5 ml (⅙ fl oz) spoon
Imperial and metric measurements have
been given in all recipes. Use one set of
measurements only and not a mixture
of both.

CONTENTS

INTRODUCTION

Cooking everything in one pan, pot or tray not only saves on washing up but also reduces the time and energy you spend on cooking, which in turn helps to preserve the planet. That is why all the recipes in this book have been created so that you can just throw the ingredients together and cook away for ultimate convenience. Using one pot really is a game-changer – it has never been easier to be a *Broke Vegan*.

Each recipe makes one whole meal using a simple method and caters to vegans on a budget. Here, a light is shone on vegetables, pulses and grains as unsung heroes, rather than focusing on the expensive and overprocessed meat alternatives that are out there in force today. These ingredients are probably already to be found in the depths of your refrigerator or kitchen cupboard. Even items you might think are past their best can be salvaged to make something delicious.

These meals can be scaled back for one, prepared for you and your partner to enjoy or cooked up for family or group gatherings. Whether you want something quick to make during the week, to invest time in a more indulgent meal that takes a little longer at the weekend or to create a dish worthy of a celebration, this book has you covered.

USEFUL EQUIPMENT

- Two highly versatile pieces of equipment will get you far: a heavy-based ovenproof casserole dish about 24 cm (9½ inches) in diameter and 14 cm (5½ inches) deep with a lid or a shallow ovenproof casserole dish or frying pan about 30 cm (12 inches) in diameter with a lid, along with a large roasting tray or deep baking tray about 36 x 26 cm (14 x 10½ inches). If you don't have a lid for your dish or pan, try covering it with a large baking tray weighted down with something heatproof.

- The number of bowls required for preparing different ingredients has been kept to a minimum, but in recipes where several ingredients need preparing, it is often easier to use just one large chopping board and, once prepped, leave the ingredients in little piles on the board ready to be used. In many of these cases, you will need only one cooking pan and the board.

SAVE ON WASHING UP

- You can mostly re-use prep bowls without the need to rinse them in between, as the ingredients are to be combined and cooked in one pan anyway.

- Weigh ingredients directly into the bowl you are mixing them in rather than in separate small bowls. Liquids are measured in millimetres (ml) and fluid ounces (fl oz), and if using digital scales, you can usually change the unit of measure from weight (grams or ounces) to volume and measure liquids directly in the bowl too. But even if your scales don't have this function, you can simply measure liquids in grams, as it is the same figure for both and you save using a measuring jug. Easy!

- Using a hand blender instead of a food processor, which you can do in most cases, is really helpful, as you can simply blitz away in the pan you are already using rather than transferring ingredients to the bowl of a food processor, meaning one less item to wash.

- Instead of dissolving vegan stock cubes or bouillon powder in boiling water in a separate jug, add the stock straight to the pan, making sure you give it a good stir, and then add the hot water – that way you don't have to wash up a jug that has only had hot water in it!

- Use the empty can to measure water or stock if you have just used a can of tomatoes or beans, for example.

- When you cook rice or grains for a meal, it is always worth cooking more than you need and freezing the extra portions, which can then be used in other recipes to save using more than one cooking pan.

MIDWEEK
MARVELS

HOT & SOUR NOODLE SOUP

Spicy and tangy from the chilli, vinegar and rice wine, this is like the classic Chinese takeaway dish but thickened with extra cornflour rather than an egg. Although particularly good with rice noodles, ramen or soba noodles also work well here. Feel free to throw in some greens such as pak choi, spinach or cabbage right at the end.

SERVES 4

2 tablespoons sesame oil

2 garlic cloves, finely sliced

2 cm (¾ inch) piece of ginger, peeled and grated

150 g (5 oz) shiitake mushrooms, sliced

100 g (3½ oz) oyster mushrooms, sliced

2 red chillies, deseeded and finely chopped

1.5 litres (2½ pints) vegan stock

3 tablespoons light soy sauce

4 teaspoons rice wine vinegar

1½ tablespoons Chinese Shaoxing rice wine or dry sherry

1½ tablespoons light brown sugar

½ teaspoon ground black pepper

100 g (3½ oz) rice, ramen or soba noodles

100 g (3½ oz) canned, drained sliced bamboo shoots

3 tablespoons cornflour

3 tablespoons water

salt, if needed

To serve

3 spring onions, finely sliced

lime wedges

Heat the sesame oil in a large saucepan, add the garlic and ginger and cook over a medium heat for 4 minutes. Then add all the mushrooms and the chillies and cook for about 10 minutes until the mushrooms are softened and caramelized.

Pour over the stock, soy sauce, vinegar and rice wine or sherry and sprinkle in the sugar and pepper, then simmer for 20 minutes to allow the flavours to mingle.

Stir in the noodles with the bamboo shoots and cook according to the packet instructions for your chosen noodles.

Just before the noodles are ready, mix the cornflour with the measured water until smooth, add to the soup and cook, stirring, for about 2 minutes until thickened. Taste and add salt if needed.

Serve in bowls topped with the spring onions and some lime wedges alongside.

CAULIFLOWER, CARROT & SPINACH DHAL

Who doesn't love a soothing dhal, especially when it is so easy to make. Taking inspiration from the traditional Indian dish, chunky vegetables are added to the lentils here to make it more like a stew. You can swap these vegetables quite easily; the variation below features squash and courgettes, for example. Enjoy on its own or with rotis, flatbreads or rice.

SERVES 4

2 tablespoons vegetable oil

1 tablespoon cumin seeds

1 onion, finely chopped

2.5 cm (1 inch) piece of
   ginger, peeled and grated

2 teaspoons garam masala

1 teaspoon ground coriander

300 g (10 oz) cauliflower,
   broken into small florets

300 g (10 oz) carrots, peeled
   and cut into bite-sized
   chunks

200 g (7 oz) red split lentils,
   washed and drained

750 ml (1¼ pints) water

1 teaspoon ground turmeric

1 tablespoon salt

handful of spinach, roughly
   chopped

handful of coriander leaves,
   to serve

Heat the vegetable oil in a large saucepan, add the cumin seeds and let them sizzle over a medium heat for a few seconds. Then add the onion and cook for about 8 minutes until soft and translucent. Stir in the ginger, garam masala and ground coriander and cook for another 2 minutes.

Add the vegetables and lentils and stir to coat them in the spiced onions, then pour in the measured water. Bring to a simmer and cook gently for 20 minutes.

Skim off any residue on the surface of the liquid, then stir in the turmeric and salt and cook for another 15 minutes, or until the vegetables and lentils are tender.

Stir the spinach through the lentil mixture and cook for 2 minutes until wilted. Serve in bowls topped with the coriander leaves.

FOR SQUASH & COURGETTE DHAL, swap the cauliflower and carrots for 300 g (10 oz) peeled and deseeded squash and 300 g (10 oz) courgettes, both cut into large chunks. Keep the spinach if you want more greens or omit – it is entirely up to you!

MISO VEGETABLE & PASTA SOUP

A hearty soup that draws on the classic Italian minestrone for its main components, its flavour is emboldened with umami from the miso paste. Give yourself a pat on the back for getting so many vegetables into one bowl!

SERVES 4-6

3 tablespoons olive oil, plus
  extra for drizzling
1 large onion, finely chopped
2 carrots, peeled and
  finely chopped
2 celery sticks, finely
  chopped
2 garlic cloves, crushed
2 litres (3½ pints) water
2 tablespoons white miso
  paste
100 g (3½ oz) spaghetti,
  broken into small pieces
2 courgettes, cut into
  small chunks
½ hispi (sweetheart)
  cabbage, finely shredded
4 tomatoes, cut into small
  chunks
200 g (7 oz) asparagus
  spears, cut into 1 cm
  (½ inch) thick slices on
  the diagonal
400 g (13 oz) can borlotti
  or haricot beans, drained
  and rinsed
finely grated zest and juice
  of 1 lemon
salt and pepper

Heat the olive oil in a large saucepan, add the onion, carrots, celery and garlic and cook over a medium heat for about 8 minutes until the onion is soft and translucent.

Pour over the measured water, add the miso paste and stir to dissolve. Bring to a simmer, add the spaghetti and cook for 5 minutes. Stir in the courgettes and cabbage and cook for another 5 minutes.

Add the tomatoes, asparagus, beans, lemon zest and juice, and salt and pepper to taste and cook for another 2 minutes. Add more water if you prefer it more brothy.

Serve in bowls, drizzled with olive oil and topped with extra salt and pepper.

RATATOUILLE GRATIN

This rich vegetable medley features many of the same components as the famed slow-cooked Provençal dish ratatouille, but is simple and relatively quick to prepare with a crunchy zesty topping. You can change up the vegetables easily here, by using leeks and fennel instead (see below).

SERVES 2–4

2 red onions, finely sliced
1 red pepper, sliced
1 yellow pepper, sliced
1 courgette, sliced
2 large tomatoes, cut into
   wedges
olive oil
leaves from 2 thyme sprigs
100 g (3½ oz) tomato passata
1 tablespoon sherry vinegar
4 garlic cloves, crushed
salt and pepper
handful of parsley leaves,
   chopped, to serve

Breadcrumb topping
100 g (3½ oz) panko or fresh
   breadcrumbs
finely grated zest of 1 lemon
2 tablespoons olive oil
salt and pepper

Preheat the oven to 200°C (400°F), Gas Mark 6.

Toss together all the vegetables, a few tablespoons of olive oil, the thyme leaves, passata, vinegar and some salt and pepper in a large ovenproof dish. Cook in the oven for 30 minutes until the vegetables are lightly golden around the edges.

Meanwhile, mix together the breadcrumb topping ingredients in a small bowl.

Stir the garlic into the vegetable mixture and then sprinkle the breadcrumbs over the top. Return to the oven and cook for 10–12 minutes until the topping is golden brown.

Scatter over the parsley and serve.

FOR LEEK & FENNEL GRATIN, cut 4 large leeks into 5 cm (2 inch) lengths and place in a large ovenproof dish with 3 fennel bulbs (tough outer layers and stalks removed, cut into thin wedges). Add 2 tablespoons olive oil, 4 finely sliced garlic cloves, leaves from 3 thyme sprigs and some salt and pepper. Pour over 200 ml (7 fl oz) vegan white wine and 200 ml (7 fl oz) vegan stock. Cook in the oven at 200°C (400°F) for 30 minutes until the vegetables are nicely braised. Add the breadcrumb topping and bake as for the Ratatouille Gratin, then scatter over some parsley leaves and serve.

CAULIFLOWER & WHITE BEAN SOUP

Such a comforting bowl of creamy soup, thickened with beans, flavoured with rosemary and topped with crispy fried rosemary sprigs. Try making it using a head of broccoli instead for an equally delicious result (see below).

SERVES 4-6

2 tablespoons olive oil, plus
    extra for drizzling
1 tablespoon finely chopped
    rosemary, plus a few extra
    small sprigs for frying
    to serve
2 leeks, thoroughly washed
    and finely sliced
2 celery sticks, finely
    chopped
1 carrot, peeled and finely
    chopped
3 garlic cloves, crushed
1 large cauliflower, broken
    into florets and stalk cut
    into small chunks
400 g (13 oz) can cannellini
    or butter beans
1.5 litres (2½ pints) vegan
    stock
salt and pepper
a few gratings of nutmeg,
    to serve

Heat the olive oil in a large saucepan, add the rosemary sprigs and fry until crisp. Remove with a slotted spoon and leave to drain on a plate lined with kitchen paper.

Add the leeks, celery, carrot, chopped rosemary and garlic to the oil left in the pan and cook over a medium heat for about 8 minutes until the vegetables are softened but not coloured too much.

Add the cauliflower, beans and their liquid from the can and stock and bring to a simmer. Cook for about 30 minutes until the cauliflower is soft.

Use a hand blender to blitz the soup until smooth, adding a little more water if it is too thick, and season with salt and pepper to taste.

Ladle into bowls, then drizzle with olive oil, add a grinding of pepper and the nutmeg and top with the crispy rosemary sprigs.

FOR BROCCOLI & BEAN SOUP, swap the cauliflower for a large head of broccoli. Feel free to change up the beans and herbs to create different flavours. Borlotti or flageolet beans are really delicious if you can get hold of them, and thyme and parsley work well too.

CUMIN-SPICED CARROT, PARSNIP & LENTIL STEW

Easy to whip up, this delicious stew is mildly spiced, lightly caramelized and freshened with mint and parsley. Use bunched carrots with their leafy green tops intact if you can find them, as the greens bring another flavour element to the dish besides looking great. Now you know, why would you ever throw them away?

SERVES 2–4

300 g (10 oz) carrots,
    preferably with green leafy
    tops, peeled and cut into
    long wedges, tops roughly
    chopped
200 g (7 oz) parsnips, peeled
    and cut into long wedges
1 red onion, sliced
1 tablespoon cumin seeds
1 tablespoon maple syrup
2 tablespoons olive oil
250 g (8 oz) pack
    ready-cooked Puy lentils
200 ml (7 fl oz) vegan stock
handful of mint leaves,
    roughly chopped
handful of parsley leaves,
    roughly chopped
salt and pepper

Preheat the oven to 200°C (400°F), Gas Mark 6.

Toss together the carrots, parsnips, onion, cumin seeds, maple syrup, a generous pinch of salt and pepper and the olive oil in a large roasting tray.

Roast for about 30 minutes until the vegetables are cooked and are slightly caramelized from the maple syrup.

Stir in the lentils and stock and return to the oven for another 10 minutes just until the lentils are infused with the cumin flavour.

Stir through the herbs, and carrot tops if you have them, and serve.

LEMONY COURGETTE ORZO

A light and easy meal to make for lunch or dinner, the courgette is barely cooked to add a bit of texture to the very soft and almost buttery orzo grains.

SERVES 2

2 tablespoons olive oil,
   plus extra for drizzling
1 onion, finely chopped
2 garlic cloves, crushed
150 g (5 oz) orzo
500 ml (17 fl oz) hot vegan
   stock
2 large courgettes, cut into
   thin strips or coarsely
   grated
finely grated zest and juice
   of 1 lemon
¼ teaspoon chilli flakes
salt and pepper
8 basil leaves, to serve

Heat the olive oil in a medium-sized saucepan or large frying pan, add the onion and cook over a medium heat for about 8 minutes until soft and translucent. Add the garlic and cook for another 2 minutes.

Stir in the orzo, pour in the hot stock and simmer for 10 minutes until the orzo is cooked but with a slight bite to it.

Add the courgettes, lemon zest and juice and chilli flakes. If the orzo has absorbed all the liquid, add a little water until it is the consistency you prefer. Simmer for 2 minutes, then season with salt and pepper to taste.

Serve in bowls, drizzled with olive oil and topped with the basil leaves.

FOR FENNEL & LEEK ORZO, swap the courgette, onion and basil for leek, fennel fronds and seeds. Heat the olive oil in a medium-sized saucepan or large frying pan, add 1 finely sliced leek, 2 finely sliced garlic cloves and 1 fennel bulb (tough outer layers and stalks removed, reserving the fronds). Cook over a medium heat for about 10 minutes until the fennel is tender. Add the fennel seeds, orzo and stock, then cook and serve as for Lemony Courgette Orzo but topped with the fennel fronds.

FOR PEA & SPINACH ORZO, put the orzo in a medium-sized saucepan or large frying pan, pour in 400 ml (14 fl oz) of the hot vegan stock and simmer for 5 minutes. Meanwhile, put 150 g (5 oz) defrosted frozen peas, the remaining 100 ml (3 ½ fl oz) stock and 50 g (2 oz) roughly chopped spinach in a blender and blitz until you have a smooth purée. Add the spinach blend to the orzo with an additional 150 g (5 oz) peas and 50 g (2 oz) spinach and cook for another 5 minutes. Season and then stir in the zest and juice of 1 lemon with ¼ teaspoon chilli flakes.

BAKED TOMATO & GARLIC GNOCCHI

This is a great way to cook shop-bought gnocchi. It crisps up beautifully, adding an extra dimension to the texture, while absorbing the flavours from the roasted vegetables. And it is all done in one tray.

SERVES 4

625 g (1¼ lb) cherry or baby
  plum tomatoes, halved
6 garlic cloves, unpeeled
large pinch of chilli flakes
2 tablespoons olive oil, plus
  extra for drizzling
2 thyme sprigs
500 g (1 lb) pack
  shop-bought gnocchi
salt and pepper
handful of basil leaves,
  to serve

Preheat the oven to 200°C (400°F), Gas Mark 6.

Toss together the tomatoes, garlic cloves, chilli flakes, a large pinch of salt and pepper and the olive oil in a large roasting tray. Strip the leaves off the thyme sprigs and scatter over, then throw in the stalks for added flavour. Roast for 20 minutes.

Stir in the gnocchi and roast for another 30 minutes until the tomatoes are soft and the gnocchi is lightly coloured.

Use the back of a spoon to squeeze the soft roasted garlic out of the skins, discarding the skins, and give everything a final stir. Taste and adjust the seasoning, drizzle with olive oil and scatter over the basil leaves.

FOR BUTTERNUT SQUASH & SAGE GNOCCHI, swap the tomatoes for 500 g (1 lb) peeled and deseeded butternut squash, cut into 1 cm (½ inch) thick slices. Roast for 20 minutes with the chilli flakes, salt, pepper and olive oil until the squash has started to soften and turned golden brown around the edges. Stir in the gnocchi with 6 roughly chopped sage leaves and 3 crushed garlic cloves. Add another drizzle of oil if needed and roast for another 30 minutes.

FOR MIXED MUSHROOM GNOCCHI, use 400 g (13 oz) mixed mushrooms, such as chestnut, portobellini or closed cup, left whole if small, or quartered if large. Roast the mushrooms tossed with the leaves of 2 rosemary sprigs, along with salt, pepper and olive oil for 20 minutes as above. Stir in the gnocchi with 3 crushed garlic cloves and roast for another 30 minutes. Stir through a large handful of roughly chopped parsley leaves and drizzle with olive oil before serving.

WARM POTATO, RADISH & CARROT SALAD

Potatoes roasted with sweet, citrusy coriander seeds and aniseedy fennel seeds are a real, warming treat. Throw in some radishes, carrots and spinach and you have a vibrant and delicious meal to savour.

SERVES 2-4

500 g (1 lb) baby potatoes, halved
300 g (10 oz) baby carrots, left whole, or large carrots, peeled and cut into batons
olive oil
1 tablespoon coriander seeds
1 tablespoon fennel seeds
300 g (10 oz) radishes, halved
100 g (3½ oz) peashoots
salt and pepper

To serve
juice of ½ lemon
2 tablespoons roughly chopped chives

Preheat the oven to 200°C (400°F), Gas Mark 6.

Toss together the potatoes, carrots, a generous drizzle of olive oil, some salt and pepper and the coriander and fennel seeds in a large roasting tray. Roast for about 30 minutes until the potatoes are cooked through and crispy.

Add the radishes, give everything a stir and roast for another 20 minutes.

Take the tray out of the oven, mix in the peashoots and leave until wilted from the heat. Squeeze over the lemon juice, scatter over the chives and serve.

COURGETTE & AUBERGINE FARINATA

The pancake featured here made using gram (chickpea) flour is inspired by the Italian farinata, which is usually served alongside vegetables. But in this all-in-one method, the vegetables are combined with the batter much like a big vegan frittata.

SERVES 4–6

1 aubergine, cut into 1 cm
   (½ inch) thick rounds
1 courgette, halved
   lengthways and cut into
   1 cm (½ inch) thick
   half-moons on the diagonal
2 garlic cloves, finely sliced
leaves from 2 rosemary
   sprigs, roughly chopped
olive oil
salt and pepper
handful of parsley leaves,
   roughly chopped

Pancake batter
200 g (7 oz) gram (chickpea)
   flour
pinch of salt and pepper
475 ml (16 fl oz) warm water
2 tablespoons olive oil

Preheat the oven to 200°C (400°F), Gas Mark 6.

First make the pancake batter. Whisk together the flour and salt and pepper in a bowl, then make a well in the centre. Pour the warm water and olive oil into the well and whisk until you have a smooth batter. Set aside.

Toss together the vegetables, garlic, rosemary, some salt and pepper and a generous drizzle of olive oil in shallow casserole dish, approximately 30 cm (12 inches) in diameter, preferably nonstick, and roast for 30 minutes until lightly coloured.

Give the vegetables a stir so that none are stuck to the bottom of the dish, add another drizzle of olive oil and then pour over the batter, ensuring it is evenly spread out.

Bake for about 20 minutes until the pancake is firm to the touch. Scatter over the parsley leaves and serve.

FOR RED PEPPER, TOMATO & CHILLI FARINATA, make the pancake batter as above. Swap the aubergine, courgette, and rosemary for 1 red pepper, sliced into strips, 200 g (7 oz) cherry tomatoes, halved, and 2 red chillies, deseeded and finely chopped. Toss with some salt and pepper and olive oil and roast for 30 minutes, then pour over the batter and bake as above. Scatter over a handful of parsley leaves, roughly chopped, to serve.

SHIITAKE CRISPY GARLIC CONGEE

Congee, Chinese rice porridge, is a classic breakfast dish and the ultimate soothing comfort food. This simple savoury porridge can, however, be served for any meal of the day, with the toppings changed up for extra versatility. It takes a little while to cook, but once you have the rice underway it can be left to its own devices.

SERVES 4

2 tablespoons sesame oil
4 garlic cloves, finely sliced
200 g (7 oz) shiitake
    mushrooms, sliced
200 g (7 oz) jasmine rice,
    quickly rinsed (you do
    not want to get rid of too
    much of the starch)
3 cm (1¼ inch) piece of
    ginger, peeled and finely
    grated
1.65 litres (2¾ pints) hot
    vegan stock
salt and pepper

To serve
light soy sauce
3 spring onions, finely sliced

Heat the sesame oil in a large saucepan, add the garlic and fry over a medium heat until golden brown and crispy. Remove with a slotted spoon and leave to drain on a plate lined with kitchen paper.

Add the mushrooms to the oil left in the pan and cook for about 6–8 minutes until brown and crisp around the edges. Remove from the pan and leave to drain alongside the garlic.

Add the rice and ginger to the pan and stir until all the grains are coated in the garlicky mushroom oil. Pour over the hot stock and bring to the boil, then reduce the heat and simmer, uncovered, for about 1 hour, stirring occasionally, until thickened and the rice is broken up and soft.

Season with salt and pepper to taste and stir in half the mushrooms and half the crispy garlic. If the porridge is too thick (it will thicken as it cools down), add more stock or water to achieve your desired consistency.

Ladle into bowls and top with the remaining mushrooms and crispy garlic, a few dashes of soy sauce and the spring onions.

BRAISED LITTLE GEM LETTUCE & NOODLES

Even when cooked, lettuce still holds a slight crunch to it. Paired with miso broth and some chilli kick, this is a really delicious way to use up lettuce in the refrigerator that is no longer quite crisp enough for a salad.

SERVES 4

2 tablespoons sesame oil

2 garlic cloves, crushed

2 cm (¾ inch) piece of ginger, peeled and grated

4 Little Gem lettuces, quartered

2 tablespoons white miso paste, dissolved in 500 ml (17 fl oz) water

100 g (3½ oz) rice vermicelli noodles

150 g (5 oz) frozen peas

salt and pepper

To serve

4 spring onions, finely sliced

chilli oil, to taste

Heat the sesame oil in a shallow casserole dish, add the garlic and ginger and fry over a medium heat for about 2 minutes until soft.

Arrange the lettuce quarters in the oil, one cut side down, and cook until crispy and golden on that side, then turn so that the other cut side is facing down and cook in the same way – this should take about 5–8 minutes in total.

Remove the lettuce quarters and set aside on the chopping board that you used for preparing the ingredients.

Pour the miso mixture into the dish and bring to a gentle simmer. Add the rice noodles, stir gently and cook for 2 minutes until softened, then add the peas and the lettuce quarters and cook for another 2 minutes. Add more water if you prefer it more brothy and season with salt and pepper to taste.

Ladle into bowls, top with the spring onions and add a drizzle of chilli oil to taste.

EDAMAME FRIED RICE

Once you have all the ingredients ready, this is a really fast and easy dinner, whipped up in minutes. Full of flavour and textures, it is a brilliant way to jazz up leftover rice.

SERVES 4

2 tablespoons sesame oil

3 garlic cloves, grated

2.5 cm (1 inch) piece of
    ginger, peeled and grated

2 carrots, peeled and finely
    chopped

700 g (1 lb 6 oz) leftover
    cooked white rice,
    preferably long-grain
    or basmati

250 g (8 oz) frozen or fresh
    podded edamame beans

2 tablespoons tamari or light
    soy sauce

2 tablespoons hoisin sauce

salt (optional)

Quick-pickled radishes

100 g (3½ oz) radishes,
    finely sliced

50 ml (2 fl oz) rice wine
    vinegar

pinch of sugar

pinch of salt

To serve

3 spring onions, finely sliced
    on the diagonal

50 g (2 oz) shop-bought
    crispy fried onions

First make the quick-pickled radishes. Add all the ingredients to a small bowl and stir to combine. Set aside while you make the fried rice.

Heat the sesame oil in a large wok or frying pan, add the garlic and ginger and fry over a medium to high heat for about 1 minute until golden.

Add the carrots and stir-fry for about 3 minutes until slightly softened. Stir in the rice, breaking up any clumps with a spoon, and keep stirring with the ingredients in the pan.

Add the edamame beans, tamari or soy sauce and hoisin and stir until everything is evenly coated in the sauces. Cook for another 5 minutes until the beans are bright green.

Add salt to taste if needed (the sauces should make the dish salty enough), then serve in bowls topped with the quick-pickled radishes, spring onions and crispy fried onions.

FOR CASHEW NUT & PINEAPPLE FRIED RICE, cook as above but stir-fry 200 g (7 oz) cashew nuts with the carrots so that they are lightly toasted. Add 200 g (7 oz) fresh pineapple chunks, 1 tablespoon rice wine vinegar and a pinch of sugar, then add the rice and sauces (omitting the edamame beans) and continue cooking as above. Serve with sriracha sauce if you like a bit of heat.

GARLICKY BROTHY BEANS WITH RAINBOW CHARD

Simple and quick, this is perfect for a laid-back lunch or casual dinner. You can use whatever canned beans you fancy – it is also really good with chickpeas (see below) – and whatever veg you have in the refrigerator.

SERVES 2

2 tablespoons olive oil, plus
    extra for drizzling
1 onion, finely chopped
3 garlic cloves, crushed
150 g (5 oz) rainbow chard,
    stalks cut into 1 cm
    (½ inch) thick slices and
    leaves roughly chopped
400 g (13 oz) can cannellini
    or other beans
finely grated zest and juice of
    1 lemon
500 ml (17 fl oz) vegan stock
salt and pepper

Heat the olive oil in a medium-sized saucepan, add the onion and cook over a medium heat for at least 8 minutes until softened.

Stir in the garlic and chard stalks and cook for another 2 minutes.

Add the beans and their liquid from the can, the lemon zest and juice and stock. Season with salt and pepper to taste. Bring to a simmer, then add the chard leaves and cook for 2 minutes.

Serve in bowls, drizzled with olive oil and topped with a grinding of pepper.

FOR GARLICKY BROTHY CHICKPEAS WITH TOMATO & CHILLI, cook the onion as above but add 250 g (8 oz) cherry tomatoes, halved, and 1 red chilli, deseeded and finely chopped, to the saucepan with the garlic in place of the chard stalks. Cook the tomatoes down over a medium heat for 8 minutes. Swap the cannellini beans and lemon zest and juice for a 400 g (13 oz) can chickpeas, with their liquid, along with the vegan stock. Bring to a simmer (omitting the chard leaves) and cook for 2 minutes. Season to taste before serving as above.

BLISTERED GREENS WITH HAZELNUT DRESSING

A quick blast in searing hot heat is all these veggies need to get that deliciously charred flavour. This paired with a sweet toasty hazelnut dressing makes a fabulous warm salad.

SERVES 4

100 g (3½ oz) blanched
   hazelnuts
250 g (8 oz) green beans
250 g (8 oz) Tenderstem
   broccoli
250 g (8 oz) asparagus
   spears
olive oil
finely grated zest of 1 lemon
large pinch of chilli flakes
2 tablespoons roughly
   chopped dill fronds
2 tablespoons roughly
   chopped parsley leaves
salt and pepper

Dressing
3 tablespoons wholegrain
   mustard
1½ tablespoons apple cider
   vinegar
1 tablespoon maple syrup
75 ml (3 fl oz) olive oil
generous pinch of salt
   and pepper

Preheat the oven to 200°C (400°F), Gas Mark 6.

Spread the hazelnuts out in a large roasting tray and roast for about 10 minutes until golden brown. Carefully tip the nuts on to a chopping board and leave to cool.

Increase the oven temperature to 240°C (475°F), Gas Mark 9.

Toss together all the green vegetables, a generous drizzle of olive oil, salt and pepper, the lemon zest and chilli flakes in the roasting tray and roast for 15–20 minutes until both charred and bright green.

Meanwhile, roughly chop the cooled roasted hazelnuts. Whisk together all the dressing ingredients in a small bowl.

Drizzle the dressing over the warm greens and scatter with the toasted hazelnuts and herbs before serving.

WEEKEND WONDERS

SLOW-COOKED SWEET PEPPER STEW

Based on the classic rustic Italian dish of peperonata, this rich stew of peppers, onions, tomatoes and herbs is so delicious piled on toast rubbed with olive oil and garlic. Opt out of the chilli flakes if you don't like too much heat.

SERVES 2–4

5 tablespoons olive oil, plus an extra (optional) drizzle to serve

2 onions, finely sliced

4 garlic cloves, crushed

1 red pepper, sliced into thin strips

1 yellow pepper, sliced into thin strips

1 orange pepper, sliced into thin strips

4 plum tomatoes, roughly chopped

½ teaspoon chilli flakes

finely grated zest and juice of 1 lemon

1 tablespoon sherry vinegar

1 tablespoon roughly chopped oregano leaves

handful of basil leaves

salt and pepper

Heat the olive oil in a shallow casserole dish or large frying pan with a lid, add the onions and garlic and fry over a medium heat for about 8 minutes until the onions are softened.

Add the peppers, tomatoes, chilli flakes and salt and pepper to taste and cook for about 5 minutes until the peppers have softened slightly.

Cover the pan with the lid, reduce the heat and cook slowly, stirring occasionally, for 45 minutes until the peppers, tomatoes and onions are super soft and slightly caramelized.

Stir in the lemon zest and juice, vinegar, herbs and a drizzle of olive oil, if you like, before serving.

COURGETTE & ARTICHOKE ARROZ

Imagine cooking this over an open fire by the sea in Spain, as this is a Broke Vegan *take on a paella, using turmeric to echo the original's characteristic saffron yellow colour at a fraction of the cost. The key is not to stir the rice during cooking, as you want a crispy bottom. You can change it up by using different vegetables (see below) – it is also really good with fennel, sun-dried tomatoes and olives.*

SERVES 4–6

2 tablespoons olive oil
1 onion, finely sliced
1 red pepper, finely sliced
2 garlic cloves, finely sliced
2 large courgettes, halved
    lengthways and cut into
    1 cm (½ inch) thick
    half-moons
2 tablespoons tomato purée
½ teaspoon ground turmeric
250 g (8 oz) paella rice (I use
    bomba)
750 ml (1¼ pints) hot vegan
    stock
200 g (7 oz) shop-bought
    chargrilled artichokes
salt and pepper

To serve
handful of flat leaf parsley
    leaves, roughly chopped
1 lemon, sliced into wedges

Preheat the oven to 200°C (400°F), Gas Mark 6.

Heat the olive oil in a large, shallow ovenproof casserole dish, add the onion, red pepper and garlic and cook over a medium heat for about 8 minutes until soft and beginning to caramelize.

Stir in the courgettes and cook for another 5 minutes.

Add the tomato purée, turmeric and rice, then pour over the hot stock and stir until well combined. Season with salt and pepper to taste. Arrange the artichokes on top, then cook, uncovered, in the oven for about 35 minutes until the rice is fluffy and crisp on top and most of the liquid has been absorbed.

Scatter over the parsley and serve with the lemon wedges.

FOR SUN-DRIED TOMATO & PEA ARROZ, cook as above but add 1 yellow pepper, finely sliced, along with the red pepper. Swap the courgettes and artichokes for 300 g (10 oz) frozen peas and 200 g (7 oz) sun-dried tomatoes, adding them with the tomato purée, turmeric and rice before pouring over the stock. Serve as above.

BLISSFUL BEETROOT & BLACK BEAN GOULASH

An earthy, smoky stew that takes its flavour inspiration from the classic Hungarian dish of goulash, this is easy to prepare, involving not much more than throwing all the ingredients together and letting your cooker do most of the work.

SERVES 4

2 tablespoons olive oil
2 onions, finely chopped
1 carrot, peeled and finely chopped
1 celery stick, finely chopped
4 garlic cloves, crushed
1 tablespoon caraway seeds
1 tablespoon smoked paprika
625 g (1¼ lb) beetroot, peeled and cut into 2.5 cm (1 inch) cubes
300 g (10 oz) sweet potato, peeled and cut into 2.5 cm (1 inch) cubes
400 g can (13 oz) black beans, drained and rinsed
400 g can (13 oz) chopped tomatoes
2 tablespoons tomato purée
750 ml (1¼ pints) vegan stock
salt and pepper

To serve
2 tablespoons roughly chopped dill fronds
dairy-free crème fraîche or soured cream (optional)

Heat the olive oil in a large casserole dish with a lid, add the onions, carrot, celery and garlic and cook over a medium heat for about 8 minutes until the vegetables are soft.

Stir in the caraway seeds and smoked paprika and cook for another 2 minutes.

Add the beetroot, sweet potato, black beans, tomatoes, tomato purée and stock, and season with salt and pepper to taste. Bring to the boil, then reduce the heat, cover with the lid and cook slowly for 1 hour, stirring every 20 minutes or so.

Remove the lid and cook, uncovered, for another 20 minutes until reduced and thickened.

Serve in bowls sprinkled with the dill and topped with a dollop of dairy-free crème fraîche or soured cream, if you like.

VEGEREE

Based on the breakfast/brunch favourite kedgeree, which is traditionally made with smoked fish, this delicious all-plant rice dish can be eaten for any meal of the day. I like mine served with a squeeze of fresh lemon, some mango chutney and a dollop of dairy-free crème fraîche or soured cream.

SERVES 4

2 tablespoons olive oil

2 onions, finely sliced

2 celery sticks, finely chopped

2 garlic cloves, crushed

2 cm (¾ inch) piece of ginger, peeled and grated

4 cardamom pods, lightly crushed

2 tablespoons curry powder

½ teaspoon smoked paprika

½ teaspoon ground turmeric

240 g (7¾ oz) basmati rice, thoroughly washed and drained

100 g (3½ oz) sultanas

2 bay leaves

600 ml (1 pint) vegan stock

200 g (7 oz) spinach

200 g (7 oz) frozen peas

salt and pepper

To serve

1 tablespoon roughly chopped coriander leaves

2 tablespoons toasted flaked almonds

Heat the olive oil in a large casserole dish with a lid, add the onions and celery and cook over a medium heat for about 8 minutes until softened.

Stir in the garlic, ginger and cardamom pods and cook for another 2 minutes until the cardamom seeds pop and release their aroma.

Add the remaining spices along with the rice, sultanas and bay leaves and stir until all the grains are coated in the spice mixture. Pour over the stock and bring to a simmer, then reduce the heat, cover with the lid and cook gently for 20 minutes, stirring occasionally, until the rice is perfectly cooked and the stock has been fully absorbed.

Stir through the spinach and peas and cook gently for about 2 minutes until the spinach is wilted and the peas are bright green. Season with salt and pepper to taste, and scatter over the coriander and flaked almonds before serving.

FOR FRAGRANT BASMATI WITH GREEN BEANS & MANGO, prepare and cook the rice as above but after 15 minutes' cooking, add 250 g (8 oz) green beans, halved. Replace the lid and continue cooking until the rice is ready, then stir through 200 g (7 oz) mango, peeled and cut into 1 cm (½ inch) cubes, instead of the spinach and peas. Season and serve as above.

PEANUT BUTTER & BANANA PEEL CURRY

Bananas peels are delicious after soaking in water and cooking – an amazing way to use up something that would normally be thrown away.

SERVES 4

4 banana skins
2 tablespoons vegetable oil
12 curry leaves
1 teaspoon cumin seeds
2 onions, finely sliced
3 garlic cloves, finely sliced
2 cm (¾ inch) piece of ginger, peeled and grated
handful of coriander, stalks finely chopped, leaves reserved to serve
1 teaspoon ground turmeric
½ teaspoon chilli powder
3 heaped tablespoons smooth or crunchy peanut butter
400 ml (14 fl oz) can coconut milk
250 ml (8 fl oz) water
juice of 1 lime
1 tablespoon light brown sugar
salt

Fill a bowl with warm water, add a pinch of salt and stir to dissolve. Add the banana skins and leave to soak for a minimum of 30 minutes and up to 6 hours. Drain the banana skins and cut into thin strips.

Heat the vegetable oil in a large saucepan or deep frying pan, add the curry leaves and cumin seeds and fry over a medium heat for about 20 seconds. Then add the onions, garlic, ginger and coriander stalks and cook for about 5–8 minutes until the onions are softened.

Add the banana skin slices and cook for another 8 minutes.

Stir in the spices and cook for 1 minute, then add the peanut butter, breaking up any clumps with the back of the spoon. Pour in the coconut milk, measured water and lime juice, add the sugar and stir to combine. Bring to a simmer, then reduce the heat and cook gently for about 30 minutes until the sauce has thickened. Thin with extra water if it becomes too thick. Season with salt to taste.

Serve scattered with the coriander leaves.

FOR PEANUT BUTTER AUBERGINE CURRY, swap the banana peels for 4 aubergines, cut into 4 cm (1½ inch) chunks. Sprinkle with a little salt and leave for a couple of minutes, then pat dry with kitchen paper. First, heat 4 tablespoons vegetable oil in the pan, add the aubergine in batches and fry for about 6–8 minutes until browned. Drain on a plate lined with kitchen paper and set aside while you cook the sauce base in the pan as above. Once you have added the coconut milk, water, lime juice and sugar, stir in the fried aubergines and continue as above.

CHICKPEA SOUP & DUMPLINGS

A really lovely broth with hints of cumin and lemon is topped with soft gram (chickpea) flour dumplings, offering a handy wheat-free alternative to classic dumplings.

SERVES 4

2 tablespoons olive oil

1 onion, finely chopped

1 carrot, peeled and finely
   chopped

2 celery sticks, finely chopped

3 garlic cloves, crushed

1 teaspoon ground cumin

½ teaspoon ground turmeric

2 bay leaves

750 ml (1¼ pints) vegan stock

400 g (13 oz) can chickpeas,
   drained and rinsed

finely grated zest and juice
   of 1 lemon

½ teaspoon celery salt
   (or ordinary salt)

salt and pepper

4 tablespoons roughly
   chopped celery leaves,
   to serve

Dumplings

200 g (7 oz) gram (chickpea)
   flour

1 teaspoon baking powder

½ teaspoon celery salt
   (or ordinary salt)

½ teaspoon ground black
   pepper

100 ml (3½ fl oz) oat milk

100 ml (3½ fl oz) water

Heat the olive oil in a medium-sized saucepan with a lid, add the onion, carrot, celery and garlic and cook over a medium heat for about 8 minutes until soft, stirring often so that the vegetables do not colour too much.

Stir in the spices and cook for another 2 minutes. Add all the remaining soup ingredients, except the celery leaves, stir to combine and season with salt and pepper to taste. Bring to a gentle simmer and cook for about 10 minutes.

Meanwhile, mix together all the dry dumpling ingredients in a bowl. Make a well in the centre. Whisk together the oat milk and measured water in a jug, then mix into the dumpling mixture until you have a thick batter.

Dollop tablespoons of the dumpling batter on to the surface of the soup with a little space in between – it should make about 8–10 dumplings. Cover with the lid and cook for about 8 minutes until the dumplings are fluffy but firm.

Serve the soup and dumplings in bowls with the celery leaves scattered over.

SQUASH, SAGE & SWEET ONION PANADE

Known as panade in its traditional French form, this comforting, baked dish is a great way to use up stale bread. The key is cooking down the onions until they are sweet and soft. Try swapping the squash for mushrooms and chard for another winning combination (see page 54).

SERVES 4-6

8 tablespoons olive oil

8 slices of stale sourdough

14 sage leaves

4 onions, finely sliced

4 garlic cloves, crushed

200 ml (7 fl oz) vegan dry white wine

1 litre (1¾ pints) vegan stock

500 g (1 lb) butternut squash, peeled, deseeded and cut into 5 cm (2 inch) thick slices

salt and pepper

Heat 3 tablespoons of the olive oil in a wide, shallow ovenproof casserole dish with a lid, add the bread slices in batches and lightly fry over a medium heat for 1–2 minutes until golden on both sides. Remove with a slotted spoon and drain on a plate lined with kitchen paper.

Add the sage leaves to the oil left in the pan, adding more oil if necessary, and fry over a medium-high heat for about 15–30 seconds on each side until crisp. Remove from the pan and leave to drain alongside the fried bread.

Pour 5 tablespoons olive oil into the pan, add the onions with a pinch of salt and pepper and cook slowly over a low-medium heat for 15–20 minutes until they are soft.

Meanwhile, preheat the oven to 200°C (400°F), Gas Mark 6.

Stir the garlic into the onions and cook for another 5 minutes. Add the wine, increase the temperature to medium and cook until reduced by half, then stir in the stock. Ladle the stock and onions into a large jug.

Arrange a single layer of the fried bread over the base of the casserole dish, then ladle over some of the stock and onions. Add a few of the crisp sage leaves, breaking them up gently with your hands, and top with some of the squash slices and more stock and onions. Repeat until the layers are submerged in the stock.

Cover the pan with the lid and bake for 40 minutes, then remove the lid and bake, uncovered, for another 20 minutes until golden. Serve with any leftover crispy sage leaves.

MUSHROOM & CHARD PANADE

SERVES 4–6

30g (1 oz) dried wild
    mushrooms

8 tablespoons olive oil

8 slices of stale sourdough
    bread

500 g (1 lb) chestnut
    mushrooms, sliced

1 tablespoon thyme leaves

200 g (7 oz) chard, stalks
    sliced and leaves roughly
    chopped

3 onions, finely sliced

4 garlic cloves, crushed

200 ml (7 fl oz) vegan dry
    red wine

1 litre (1¾ pints) vegan stock,
    including the mushroom
    soaking liquid

salt and pepper

Put the dried mushrooms in a jug, pour over boiling water to cover and leave to soak for 30 minutes. Strain through a fine sieve, adding the soaking liquid to the stock to make up the required quantity.

Fry the bread slices in 3 tablespoons of olive oil in the casserole dish for 1–2 minutes on each side until golden brown, then drain as for the Squash, Sage & Sweet Onion Panade (see page 52).

Fry the soaked dried and chestnut mushrooms together in batches in the oil left in the pan, along with a generous pinch of salt and pepper and the thyme leaves, for about 6–8 minutes. Once cooked, pile on to a large chopping board or plate.

Add the chard to the pan and cook briefly just until wilted. Transfer to the board or plate in a separate pile.

Gently fry the onions and then the garlic in 5 tablespoons of olive oil in the pan as before, then add and reduce the red wine by half before stirring in the stock.

Layer up the casserole dish with the fried bread, stock and onions, mushrooms and chard and bake as on page 52.

SMOKY BLACK BEAN CHILLI WITH CORNBREAD TOPPING

A whole meal in one, this deeply flavoured chilli is almost meaty in texture with the use of black beans and baked complete with its own accompaniment in the form of a fluffy golden cornbread topping.

SERVES 4–6

1 tablespoon olive oil
1 large red onion, finely chopped
3 garlic cloves, crushed
2 celery sticks, finely chopped
1 red pepper, finely chopped
1 green pepper, finely chopped
1 yellow pepper, finely chopped
2 x 400 g (13 oz) cans black beans, drained and rinsed
400 g (13 oz) can chopped tomatoes
1 tablespoon tomato purée
1½ teaspoons smoked paprika
1 teaspoon ground cumin
½ teaspoon cayenne pepper
½ teaspoon ground cinnamon
2 bay leaves
salt and pepper

Cornbread topping

150 g (5 oz) plain flour
150 g (5 oz) coarse polenta
40 g (1½ oz) caster sugar
1 tablespoon baking powder
1 teaspoon salt
1 teaspoon ground black pepper
300 ml (½ pint) dairy-free milk
75 ml (3 fl oz) vegetable oil

To serve

small handful of coriander leaves
2 limes, cut into wedges
2 avocados, halved, peeled, pitted and roughly chopped, then seasoned with salt and pepper

Preheat the oven to 180°C (350°F), Gas Mark 4.

Heat the olive oil in a large, preferably shallow (but will still work if deep) ovenproof casserole dish with a lid, add the onion, garlic and celery with a pinch of salt and cook over a medium heat for 8 minutes until the onion and celery are soft.

Add the peppers and cook for another 5 minutes.

Stir in the black beans, tomatoes, half the empty can of water, the tomato purée, spices, bay leaves and salt and pepper to taste. Bring to a simmer, then cover with the lid and cook in the oven for 2 hours.

Continued overleaf

Meanwhile, mix together all the dry cornbread topping ingredients in a large bowl, then make a well in the centre. Whisk together the wet ingredients in a jug, pour into the well and stir in the dry ingredients until you have a thick smooth batter. Set aside.

Take the dish out of the oven and remove the lid (watch out for the hot steam), then spoon large dollops of the cornbread batter evenly over the bean mixture. Bake, uncovered, for about 35 minutes until the cornbread is golden.

Serve in bowls along with the coriander leaves, lime wedges and avocado.

FOR SWEETCORN & KIDNEY BEAN CHILLI, swap the black beans for a 400 g (13 oz) can red kidney beans, drained and rinsed, and 500 g (1 lb) frozen or canned, drained sweetcorn, which makes a lighter alternative. Cook and serve as above.

AROMATIC CHICKPEA STEW

A rich, sweet stew flavoured with all the spices of a traditional Moroccan tagine, plus a sharp zing from the preserved lemons (if you can't find these, just use the finely grated zest and juice of a lemon). The sweet potatoes can easily be swapped for another vegetable, depending on what is available seasonally or best value for money, such as butternut squash, courgettes and aubergines (see below).

SERVES 4–6

2 tablespoons olive oil

2 onions, finely sliced

4 garlic cloves, crushed

2 teaspoons ground cumin

1 teaspoon ground coriander

1 teaspoon ground ginger

1 cinnamon stick

1 kg (2 lb) sweet potatoes, peeled and cut into large chunks

400 g (13 oz) can chickpeas, drained and rinsed

400 g (13 oz) can chopped tomatoes

200 g (7 oz) dates, pitted

1 preserved lemon, cut into eighths

500 ml (17 fl oz) vegan stock

½ teaspoon chilli flakes, or to taste

salt and pepper

To serve

handful of parsley leaves, roughly chopped

50 g (2 oz) toasted pine nuts

Heat the olive oil in a large casserole dish or heavy-based pan with a lid, add the onions and garlic and cook over a medium heat for about 6–8 minutes until the onions are soft and golden brown.

Stir in all the spices, except the chilli flakes, and cook for another 2 minutes.

Add the sweet potatoes, chickpeas, tomatoes, dates, preserved lemon and stock and stir until well combined. Bring to a simmer, then reduce the heat, cover with the lid and cook for about 30 minutes until the sweet potatoes are tender, stirring occasionally. Season with salt and pepper and chilli flakes to taste.

Serve scattered with the parsley and toasted pine nuts.

FOR SQUASH & COURGETTE CHICKPEA STEW, switch out the sweet potatoes and dates for 625 g (1¼ lb) butternut squash, peeled, deseeded and cut into 2 cm (¾ inch) chunks, and 2 courgettes, cut into 2 cm (¾ inch) chunks. This makes for a lighter and less sweet alternative.

FOR AUBERGINE & APRICOT CHICKPEA STEW, swap the sweet potatoes and dates for 4 aubergines, cut into 2.5 cm (1 inch) chunks, and 100 g (3½ oz) dried apricots, halved.

PLANTAIN WITH SPICY RED PEPPER & TOMATO RICE

This recipe is inspired by the flavours of the West African dish jollof rice where rice is cooked in a tomato stew with sweet, smoky and fiery Scotch bonnet chillies and red peppers. Traditionally, the tomato stew is blitzed, but here it is left chunkier for ease.

SERVES 4

4 tablespoons vegetable oil or other flavourless oil

2 large ripe plantains, peeled and halved

2 onions, finely chopped

4 garlic cloves, crushed

2.5 cm (1 inch) piece of ginger, peeled and finely grated

1–2 Scotch bonnet chillies, to taste

3 plum tomatoes, chopped

3 red peppers, cut into 3 cm (1¼ inch) pieces

2 teaspoons curry powder

5 tablespoons tomato purée

400 g (13 oz) can chopped tomatoes

3 bay leaves

240 g (7¾ oz) white long-grain rice, washed and drained

300 ml (½ pint) vegan stock

salt and pepper

large handful of parsley leaves, roughly chopped, to serve (optional)

Heat the oil in a large, heavy-based pan with a lid, add the plantain and fry for about 2–4 minutes until golden brown on all sides. Remove with a slotted spoon and leave to drain on a plate lined with kitchen paper. Sprinkle with a little salt.

Add the onions, garlic and ginger to the oil left in the pan and cook over a medium heat for about 8 minutes until soft. Then add the chillies, tomatoes and peppers and cook for another 5 minutes.

Stir in the curry powder and tomato purée until the vegetables are well coated, then mix in the tomatoes and bay leaves. Simmer for 10 minutes until most of the liquid has evaporated from the tomatoes.

Mix in the rice and stock and bring to the boil. Then reduce the heat, cover with the lid and cook gently for 25 minutes. Give the mixture a stir, then place the fried plantain on the surface of the rice, replace the lid and cook for another 20 minutes until the rice is cooked but with a slight bite to it. If it is getting too dry, add a little more stock or water.

Serve scattered with the parsley, if preferred.

CREAMY VEGETABLE COBBLER

*Cobbler doesn't have to be just a sweet dish; this is a really yummy savoury
version with herby, salty scones atop a light, creamy stew packed with
vegetables and pulses.*

SERVES 4-6

2 tablespoons olive oil

2 leeks, thoroughly washed
and finely sliced into
half-moons

4 garlic cloves, crushed

1 tablespoon dried mixed
herbs

1 heaped tablespoon plain
flour

3 large carrots, peeled and
cut into large chunks

2 parsnips, peeled and cut
into large chunks

400 g (13 oz) can cannellini
or haricot beans, drained
and rinsed

500 ml (17 fl oz) vegan stock

100 ml (3½ fl oz) oat or soya
milk

2 courgettes, cut into large
chunks

150 g (5 oz) spring greens,
shredded

handful of parsley leaves,
roughly chopped, to serve
(optional)

Cobbler topping

240 g (7¾ oz) plain flour

2 teaspoons baking powder

½ teaspoon fine salt

½ teaspoon ground black
pepper

pinch of sugar

2 teaspoons dried mixed
herbs

125 g (4 oz) cold vegan
butter, cut into small cubes

200 ml (7 fl oz) oat or soya
milk

Preheat the oven to 180°C (350°F), Gas Mark 4.

Heat the olive oil in a large ovenproof dish with a lid, add
the leeks and cook for about 5 minutes until softened.
Then add the garlic and mixed herbs and cook for another
2 minutes.

Stir in the flour, ensuring there are no lumps, and cook for
a minute or so.

Add the carrots, parsnips, beans and stock and stir well
to combine, then cover with the lid and cook in the oven
for 40 minutes.

Meanwhile, mix together all the dry cobbler topping
ingredients in a bowl. Add the vegan butter and rub
in with your fingertips until the mixture resembles
coarse breadcrumbs.

Continued overleaf

Mix in the oat or soya milk until the mixture just starts to come together into a thick batter. Cover the bowl with a clean tea towel until ready to use.

Take the dish out of the oven and increase the oven temperature to 200°C (400°F), Gas Mark 6. Remove the lid, stir in the oat or soya milk, courgettes and spring greens and then dollop heaped tablespoons of the cobbler batter on to the surface of the stew with a little space in between. Bake, uncovered, for 25–30 minutes until the cobbler topping is golden brown and risen.

Serve the cobbler scattered with the parsley, if preferred.

FOR SWEETCORN & SQUASH COBBLER, preheat the oven to 180°C (350°F), Gas Mark 4. Cook 2 onions, finely chopped, instead of the leeks, then add the garlic (omitting the mixed herbs). After mixing in the flour, add 1 butternut squash (about 1 kg/2 lb), peeled, deseeded and cut into 2 cm (¾ inch) chunks with the stock rather than the root vegetables. Cover with the lid and cook in the oven for 40 minutes. Meanwhile, make the cobbler topping as on page 62 and set aside. Remove the dish from the oven, stir in 400 g (13 oz) can sweetcorn, drained, and 2 tablespoons roughly chopped tarragon leaves with the oat or soya milk and 150g of spinach instead of spring greens and the courgettes. Bake, uncovered, for another 25–30 minutes and serve as above.

ROOT VEG & STOUT STEW WITH DUMPLINGS

A hearty, comforting stew made with stout to give it ultimate flavour and topped with fluffy little dumplings. Perfect for an evening meal during the colder months.

SERVES 4–6

2 tablespoons olive oil
2 large onions, finely sliced
150 g (5 oz) chestnut
　　mushrooms, halved
1 heaped tablespoon plain
　　flour
2 carrots, peeled and cut into
　　large chunks
2 parsnips, peeled and cut
　　into large chunks
½ swede (about 400 g/13 oz),
　　peeled and cut into large
　　chunks
½ celeriac (about 500 g/1 lb),
　　peeled and cut into large
　　chunks
150 g (5 oz) pearl barley
2 thyme sprigs
2 tablespoons dark soy sauce
2 tablespoons tomato purée
750 ml (1¼ pints) vegan stock
500 ml (17 fl oz) vegan stout
100 g (3½ oz) spinach
salt and pepper

Dumplings
150 g (5 oz) plain flour
1½ teaspoons baking powder
75 g (3 oz) vegetable suet
1 tablespoon chopped thyme
　　leaves
¼ teaspoon salt
¼ teaspoon ground black
　　pepper
100 ml (3½ fl oz) water

Heat the olive oil in a large casserole dish with a lid, add the onions and cook over a medium heat for 8 minutes until soften and translucent.

Add the mushrooms and cook for 5 minutes until lightly coloured. Then stir in the flour and cook for another minute or so.

Add all the root vegetables along with the pearl barley, thyme sprigs, soy sauce, tomato purée and a generous pinch of salt and pepper. Pour in the stock and stout and stir to combine. Bring to the boil, then reduce the heat, cover with the lid and simmer for 30 minutes.

Remove the lid and give the stew a gentle stir, then increase the heat a little and cook for another 10 minutes until the sauce is reduced and thickened.

Continued overleaf

Meanwhile, mix together all the dry dumpling ingredients, then mix in the measured water until the mixture just starts to come together into a dough. Divide the dough into 8 portions and roll into balls.

Stir the spinach into the stew and place the dumplings carefully on the surface with a little space in between, then replace the lid and cook for another 20 minutes, or until the dumplings are puffed up and firm to the touch.

BEETROOT & CASHEW CURRY

Drawing inspiration from a Sri Lankan beetroot curry, this sweet and mildly spiced dish can easily be heated up if you prefer something a little more fiery. You can also swap the beetroot for sweet potato if you prefer (see below).

SERVES 4–6

200 g (7 oz) cashew nuts

2 tablespoons coconut oil or vegetable oil

10 curry leaves

2 red onions, finely sliced

4 garlic cloves, crushed

2 green chillies, finely chopped, deseeded if you prefer less heat

2 teaspoons ground cumin

1 teaspoon ground turmeric

½ teaspoon ground coriander

2 tablespoons tomato purée

5 beetroot (total weight about 875 g/1¾ lb), peeled and cut into chunks or batons

400 ml (14 fl oz) can coconut milk

salt

Heat a casserole dish over a medium heat, add the cashews and toast for about 8 minutes, agitating them occasionally so that they are evenly coloured. Set aside (on the chopping board where you prepared the onions is ideal).

Heat the oil in the casserole dish, add the curry leaves and fry over a medium heat for about 2 minutes until they start sputtering. Stir in the onions and garlic and cook for about 8 minutes until the onions are softened. Add the chillies and cook for another 2 minutes.

Stir in the ground spices and a large pinch of salt and leave to mingle with the onions briefly before stirring in the tomato purée.

Add the beetroot and coconut milk, then fill the empty can with water and pour over. Bring to a simmer and cook for 30–40 minutes until the sauce has reduced and thickened and the beetroot is cooked but with a slight bite to it.

Stir in the toasted cashews, keeping some aside for garnish, and serve.

FOR SWEET POTATO CURRY, swap the beetroot for the same quantity of sweet potatoes, peeled and cut into 2 cm (¾ inch) chunks. You can also swap the cashews for peanuts or canned chickpeas, drained, if you fancy changing it up further.

HOPPIN' JOHN RICE

A wholesome bowl of rice and beans that takes its key ingredient pairing from the traditional Southern US dish hoppin' John, which also contains bacon or ham hock, but this is equally delicious without, served as a side dish or on its own. If you want to make this even easier, skip soaking and cooking the dried beans and just use a 400 g (13 oz) can of ready-cooked beans.

SERVES 4

250 g (8 oz) dried black-eyed beans, soaked overnight in water and then drained
2 bay leaves
1.5 litres (2½ pints) vegan stock
3 tablespoons olive oil
1 onion, finely chopped
2 celery sticks, finely chopped
3 garlic cloves, crushed
1 red pepper, finely chopped
1 green pepper, finely chopped
1 tablespoon thyme leaves
¼ teaspoon chilli flakes
¼ teaspoon cayenne pepper
125 g (4 oz) white or brown long-grain rice
salt and pepper

To serve
2 tablespoons finely chopped chives
Tabasco sauce, to taste (optional)

Put the black-eyed beans and bay leaves in a large casserole dish with a lid. Pour over the stock and bring to the boil, then reduce the heat and simmer for about 40 minutes until the beans are tender.

Drain the beans through a sieve set over a large jug, reserving the stock for later. Discard the bay leaves and set the beans aside.

Heat the olive oil in the casserole dish, add the onion, celery, garlic and peppers and cook over a medium heat for about 8 minutes until the onion is soft and translucent.

Stir in the thyme leaves, chilli flakes, cayenne and rice and cook for about 2 minutes, stirring, until all the grains and vegetables are well coated in the spices.

Pour over about 300 ml (½ pint) of the reserved stock, cover with the lid and cook for about 20 minutes until the rice is fluffy and tender and has absorbed the stock. Stir in the cooked beans and leave on the heat for a further 5 minutes to warm through. Season with salt and pepper to taste.

Serve in bowls sprinkled with the chives and seasoned with a few dashes of Tabasco sauce if you like some heat.

CARAMELIZED CABBAGE BAKED RISOTTO

You can use any cabbage here, but hispi (also known as sweetheart) cabbage is the best, as it can take a lot of cooking without losing its flavour or texture. And this recipe calls for a long caramelization in a mixture of olive oil and vegan butter before baking in the oven with risotto rice and stock. Truly delicious

SERVES 4

2 tablespoons olive oil

30 g (1 oz) vegan butter

2 onions, finely sliced

3 garlic cloves, crushed

1 hispi (sweetheart) cabbage (about 500 g/1 lb), finely shredded

2 tablespoons apple cider vinegar

250 g (8 oz) arborio risotto rice

750 ml (1¼ pints) hot vegan stock

3 thyme sprigs

handful of roughly chopped parsley, to serve (optional)

salt and pepper

Heat the olive oil and vegan butter in a large ovenproof casserole dish with a lid, add the onions with a large pinch of salt and cook over a medium heat for about 8 minutes until soft and translucent.

Add the garlic and cook for another 2 minutes. Then stir in the cabbage and vinegar and cook for another 2 minutes.

Cover the pan with the lid, reduce the heat and cook gently for 30 minutes until all the cabbage is caramelized.

Meanwhile, preheat the oven to 180°C (350°F), Gas Mark 4.

Stir the rice, hot stock, thyme sprigs and a generous pinch of salt and pepper into the pan. Replace the lid and bake for 35 minutes. Serve scattered with parsley, if preferred.

FOR CREAMY CORN BAKED RISOTTO, swap the cabbage for the kernels cut from 4 corn cobs – the best way to do this is to hold each cob in turn upright in a shallow bowl or on a chopping board and slice off the kernels with a sharp knife in downward strokes, working around the cob. (You can discard the cobs or use them to make a delicious stock.) After cooking the onions and garlic, cook the corn with the vinegar in the covered pan as above but for only 10 minutes rather than 30 minutes, along with the roughly chopped leaves from 3 tarragon sprigs. Add the rice, hot stock and seasoning, omitting the thyme. Bake as above and serve scattered with parsley, if preferred.

ENJOY TOGETHER

AUBERGINE RAGÙ

Adding aubergines – or mushrooms (see below) – to a classic Italian flavour base of onion, carrot, celery and garlic along with gutsy canned tomatoes, aromatic fennel seeds, bay leaves and chilli flakes makes an almost meaty, ragù-like pasta sauce. And here you cook the spaghetti in the sauce, so all in one pot.

SERVES 4

4 tablespoons olive oil
1 onion, finely chopped
2 carrots, peeled and finely
    chopped
2 celery sticks, finely
    chopped
2 garlic cloves, crushed
2 aubergines, cut into 1.5 cm
    (¾ inch) cubes
1 tablespoon fennel seeds
2 tablespoons tomato purée
¼ teaspoon chilli flakes
400 g (13 oz) can chopped
    tomatoes
2 bay leaves
200 g (7 oz) spaghetti
salt and pepper
handful of basil leaves,
    to serve

Heat the olive oil in a large, shallow casserole dish or deep frying pan (it is ideal if the spaghetti can lie flat on the base), add the onion, carrots, celery and garlic and cook for about 8 minutes until soft.

Add the aubergines with a large pinch of salt and cook for another 8 minutes, or until the aubergines are lightly coloured.

Stir in the fennel seeds, tomato purée and chilli flakes. Pour in the tomatoes, then fill the empty can with water twice and add to the pan along with the bay leaves and spaghetti, ensuring the pasta is entirely submerged.

Bring to a simmer and cook for about 15 minutes until the pasta is cooked but with a slight bite to it.

Season with salt and pepper to taste, give the mixture a stir and then serve scattered with the basil leaves.

FOR MUSHROOM RAGÙ, swap the aubergines for 1 kg (2 lb) mixed mushrooms (feel free to experiment with different combinations), roughly chopped, and 30 g (1 oz) dried porcini mushrooms, soaked in boiling water for 30 minutes, then strained, reserving the soaking water, and roughly chopped. The soaking water can be put towards the water measured in the empty tomato can.

BURRITO BOWL

Here, all the key elements of a burrito are simply cooked together in one pot, then served topped with a classic tomato salsa, avocado and lettuce. My Quick-pickled Radishes (see page 32) also work wonderfully with this.

SERVES 4

2 tablespoons olive oil

1 onion, finely chopped

400 g (13 oz) can pinto or borlotti beans, drained and rinsed

240 g (7¾ oz) white long-grain rice, washed and drained

1 teaspoon ground cumin

½ teaspoon chilli powder

¼ teaspoon cayenne powder

1 tablespoon tomato purée

400 g (13 oz) can chopped tomatoes

Tomato salsa & avocado topping

4 ripe tomatoes, finely chopped

1 small red onion, finely chopped

handful of coriander leaves, finely chopped, plus extra to serve

2 avocados, halved, peeled, pitted and roughly chopped

2 Little Gem lettuces, shredded

olive oil

salt and pepper

vegan soured cream (optional)

2 limes, cut into wedges

Heat the olive oil in a large saucepan with a lid, add the onion and cook over a medium heat for about 8 minutes until soft and translucent. Stir in the beans, rice, spices and tomato purée, then add the tomatoes along with half the empty can of water and a large pinch of salt and pepper. Mix to combine.

Bring to a simmer, then reduce the heat slightly, cover with the lid and cook gently for 25 minutes, or until the rice is tender and has absorbed most of the liquid. If it is too dry, add a little more water.

For the topping, combine the tomatoes with the onion and coriander for the salsa in one corner of a large chopping board. Season the avocado with salt and pepper in another corner and season the lettuce in another corner. Drizzle olive oil and squeeze a lime wedge over each pile.

Serve the rice mixture in bowls with a generous tablespoon each of the tomato salsa, avocado and lettuce. Add a dollop of vegan soured cream if preferred and scatter over the extra coriander leaves.

FOR MANGO SALSA & PICKLED CUCUMBER TOPPING, mix together 1 large peeled, pitted and finely chopped mango, 1 small finely sliced red onion, a handful of finely chopped coriander leaves, the juice of 1 lime and a generous pinch of salt and pepper. Then mix half a cucumber, thinly sliced, with 2 tablespoons vegan white wine vinegar, a pinch of light brown sugar and a pinch of salt and pepper in a separate pile on the chopping board or in a bowl. Drizzle olive oil and squeeze a lime wedge over each pile and serve as above.

MUSHROOM, CARROT & SAVOY CABBAGE LETTUCE CUPS

Inspired by the Chinese dish san choy bau, traditionally made with stir-fried pork and vegetables, the filling here uses mushrooms to achieve that savoury, umami taste, along with the classic addition of water chestnuts, readily available canned in most world food sections of supermarkets, for a lovely crunchy texture. This makes a stress-free meal for a party or gathering, as you can simply put the pan on the table and scoop the mixture into lettuce cups to serve.

SERVES 4

3 tablespoons sesame oil
1 onion, finely chopped
2 garlic cloves, thinly sliced
2.5 cm (1 inch) piece of ginger, peeled and grated or cut into thin strips
250 g (8 oz) shiitake or oyster mushrooms, roughly chopped
2 carrots, peeled and roughly chopped
¼ Savoy cabbage, finely shredded
75 g (3 oz) canned, drained water chestnuts, roughly chopped
100 g (3½ oz) bean sprouts
2 tablespoons light soy sauce
2 tablespoons hoisin sauce
2–4 Little Gem lettuces, leaves separated into 'cups'
salt and pepper

Heat the sesame oil in a wok or large saucepan, add the onion and cook over a medium to high heat for about 8 minutes until soft and golden.

Add the garlic and ginger and cook, stirring, for another 1–2 minutes. Then add the mushrooms and carrots and stir-fry for 8 minutes.

Mix in the cabbage, water chestnuts, bean sprouts and the soy and hoisin sauces with a large splash of water and cook for 2–5 minutes until the cabbage is bright green and the sauce has thickened. Season with salt and pepper to taste.

Spoon the vegetable mixture into the lettuce cups and serve immediately.

SQUASH, RED PEPPER & CHICKPEA FILO PIE

A quick and easy pie that packs a lot of flavour and looks great with its ruffled crispy top. Serve with green salad or just on its own.

SERVES 4

500 g (1 lb) butternut squash, peeled, deseeded and cut into 2 cm (¾ inch) chunks

2 red peppers, cut into thin strips

1 red onion, cut into 1 cm (½ inch) thick wedges

2 tablespoons olive oil

3 tablespoons harissa

100 g (3½ oz) tomato passata

leaves from 3 thyme sprigs

400 g (13 oz) can chickpeas, drained and rinsed

salt and pepper

Filo pastry top

6 vegan filo pastry sheets

olive oil

2 teaspoons sesame seeds

Preheat the oven to 200°C (400°F), Gas Mark 6. Put the squash, peppers and onion into a medium-sized ovenproof pie dish, add the olive oil, harissa, passata, thyme leaves, a large pinch of salt and pepper and mix to coat evenly. Cook in the oven for 30–40 minutes until the squash is tender.

Take the dish out of the oven, mix in the chickpeas and leave to cool a little while you prepare the filo pastry.

Brush each filo pastry sheet with a little olive oil and stack one on top of the other in a neat pile on a clean work top, then scrunch them up and arrange on top of the squash mixture to form a pastry lid. Drizzle with a little more olive oil and scatter over the sesame seeds. Bake for 30 minutes until the pastry is crisp and golden.

FOR SPINACH & AUBERGINE FILO PIE, cook as above but instead use 4 large aubergines cut into 2 cm (¾ inch) chunks and 1 onion, cut into 1 cm (½ inch) thick wedges. Season with salt and pepper, toss with the olive oil and cook for 30 minutes. Mix in 260g (8 ½ oz) spinach, 4 crushed garlic cloves, 2 tablespoons tahini and 2 tablespoons chopped dill fronds. Add the filo pastry top and bake as before.

FOR SPICED POTATO & PEA FILO PIE, cook as above but instead use 750 g (1 ½ lb) peeled potatoes, cut into 2 cm (¾ inch) chunks with 1 finely sliced onion. Toss with olive oil and season with salt, pepper and 1 tablespoon each of coriander seeds, cumin seeds and ground turmeric. Roast for 30–40 minutes before adding 300 g (10 oz) frozen peas and 4 crushed garlic cloves. Add the filo pastry top and bake as before.

TARTE TATIN 3 WAYS

Those unsung heroes of a roast dinner, parsnips and carrots, baked together with sweet caramelized onions under a puff pastry blanket and then upturned in the style of a Tarte Tatin, make for a real showstopper dish.

PARSNIP, CARROT & ONION TARTE TATIN

SERVES 4

4 tablespoons olive oil
3 red onions, cut into thin
    wedges
2 tablespoons light brown
    sugar
2 tablespoons vegan red
    wine vinegar
3 parsnips, peeled and cut
    into 2 cm (¾ inch) thick
    rounds, or half rounds
    if large
3 carrots, peeled and cut into
    2 cm (¾ inch) thick rounds,
    or half rounds if large
leaves from 3 thyme sprigs
320 g (11 oz) sheet ready-
    rolled vegan puff pastry
salt and pepper

Preheat the oven to 220°C (425°F), Gas Mark 7.

Heat 2 tablespoons of the olive oil in a heavy-based ovenproof frying pan about 20–23 cm (8–9 inches) in diameter, add the onions and cook over a medium heat for 10 minutes until they begin to caramelize. Sprinkle over the sugar and vinegar and cook for another 5 minutes until soft and sticky. Transfer the onions to a bowl and set aside.

Add the remaining olive oil to the pan with the parsnips, carrots, thyme leaves and some salt and pepper. Mix to coat, then roast in the oven for about 30 minutes until the vegetables begin to colour.

Meanwhile, lay out the puff pastry sheet on the clean work top and cut out a rough circle about 2.5 cm (1 inch) larger than the pan. Gently prick it all over with a fork and chill in the refrigerator until ready to use.

Take the pan out of the oven and arrange the vegetables neatly in a layer, bearing in mind that once the tart is upturned the underside of this layer will become the top. Pour over the caramelized onions, poking the wedges into the gaps between the parsnips and carrots.

Lay the pastry circle carefully over the pan and tuck in the excess pastry around the edges. Bake for about 25 minutes until the pastry is golden brown.

Ensuring your hands and wrists are protected against the heat, take the pan out of the oven, place a large plate over the top of the pan and carefully flip the tart out on to the plate. Serve warm, cut into wedges.

LEEK & WALNUT TARTE TATIN

3 large leeks (about 625 g/
   1¼ lb), cut into 3 cm
   (1¼ inch) thick rounds
2 tablespoons olive oil
2 tablespoons vegan white
   wine vinegar
2 tablespoons light brown
   sugar
100 g (3½ oz) walnut pieces
320 g (11 oz) sheet
   ready-rolled vegan
   puff pastry
salt and pepper

Preheat the oven as for the Parsnip, Carrot & Onion Tarte Tatin (see page 84). Arrange the leeks in a single layer over the base of the ovenproof frying pan, drizzle with the olive oil and season with salt and pepper, then roast for 20 minutes until golden brown.

Carefully transfer the leeks to a chopping board, keeping their shape intact as much as you can.

Place the pan over a medium heat, add the vinegar and sugar and heat until the sugar has dissolved. Add the walnuts and cook for about 2 minutes until they begin to caramelize.

Return the leek rounds to the pan, again arranging them neatly in a single layer, then add the pastry, bake and flip out on to a plate as on page 84.

BEETROOT & ROSEMARY TARTE TATIN

500 g (1 lb) beetroot, peeled
   and cut into 1 cm (½ inch)
   thick wedges
2 tablespoons olive oil
leaves from 2 rosemary
   sprigs, roughly chopped
2 tablespoons light brown
   sugar
2 tablespoons vegan red
   wine vinegar
320 g (11 oz) sheet
   ready-rolled vegan
   puff pastry
salt and pepper

Preheat the oven as for the Parsnip, Carrot & Onion Tarte Tatin (see page 84). Arrange the beetroot wedges in a single layer over the base of the ovenproof frying pan, drizzle with the olive oil, season with salt and pepper and scatter over the rosemary, then roast for 30 minutes.

Carefully transfer the beetroot to a chopping board.

Heat the sugar with the vinegar in the pan over a medium heat for 2 minutes until sugar has dissolved and is about to become caramel.

Return the beetroot to the pan, arranging it neatly in a single layer, then add the pastry, bake and flip on to a plate as on page 84.

WILD MUSHROOM & BEETROOT WELLINGTON WITH ROASTED BROCCOLI

This is a real treat, perfect for Sunday lunch or any gathering. The broccoli (or any other veg you fancy) is roasted alongside the Wellington halfway through so that you are still just using the one dish.

SERVES 4–6

2 tablespoons olive oil

2 shallots, roughly chopped

2 garlic cloves, roughly chopped

15 g (½ oz) dried wild mushrooms, soaked in boiling water for 30 minutes, strained and soaking water reserved (see page 54)

300 g (10 oz) chestnut mushrooms, roughly chopped

200 g (7 oz) green lentils, drained and rinsed

½ tablespoon light soy sauce

½ tablespoon vegan red wine vinegar

1 tablespoon thyme leaves

1 tablespoon parsley leaves, roughly chopped

25 g (1 oz) stale breadcrumbs

75 g (3 oz) ready-cooked, peeled chestnuts, roughly chopped

320 g (11 oz) sheet ready-rolled vegan puff pastry

100 g (3½ oz) spinach, slightly wilted in a microwave or with boiling hot water poured over in a sieve and excess water squeezed out

25 ml (1 fl oz) oat milk, for brushing the pastry

30 g (1 oz) black or white sesame seeds, or a mixture

salt and pepper

onion gravy (optional)

Roasted broccoli

500 g (1 lb) Tenderstem broccoli

2 tablespoons olive oil

finely grated zest of 1 lemon

Preheat the oven to 200°C (400°F), Gas Mark 6.

Heat the olive oil in a large, shallow ovenproof frying pan or casserole dish (preferably 30 cm/12 inches diameter) and fry the shallots and garlic over a medium heat. Cook for about 5 minutes until soft.

Drain and chop the wild mushrooms, reserving the soaking water. Stir the wild mushrooms into the shallot mixture, along with the chestnut mushrooms, and cook until soft. Add the lentils, soy sauce, vinegar and herbs. Season with salt and pepper to taste.

Continued overleaf

Cook the mixture for a further 5 minutes to allow the flavours to meld before turning off the heat and mixing in the breadcrumbs and the ready-cooked chestnuts. Once fully combined, scoop the mixture into a separate bowl and allow to cool completely.

Meanwhile, give the pan a wipe, so it's ready to use again. Roll out the puff pastry sheet into the pan (keeping it on its paper) and spread the spinach in an even layer in the middle, with a border of pastry around the edge.

Carefully transfer the mushroom mixture from the bowl onto the spinach and roughly form a big sausage shape. Fold in the shorter sides, then fold up the pastry margin over the filling and continue rolling up the pastry, tucking in the sides as you go, rather like a large spring roll or burrito, to encase the filling. Position the roll with the seal on the underside.

Score the top of the roll in a decorative pattern with a sharp knife, brush the pastry with oat milk and scatter over the sesame seeds. Bake in the oven for 40 minutes.

Take the Wellington out of the oven, add the broccoli to the side, drizzle over the olive oil, lemon zest and season with salt and pepper. Return to the oven for a further 15 minutes until the pastry is golden brown and the broccoli is cooked.

Slice up the Wellington and serve with onion gravy, if preferred.

BRAISED FENNEL, TOMATO & BARLEY

This is deliciously light and summery, as well as being easy to put together and have ready for a gathering. Roasting fennel in white wine really brings out its sweet aniseed flavour, and pairing it with tangy tomatoes and olives makes a well-balanced dish.

SERVES 4–6

2 fennel bulbs, any tough
    outer layers and stalks
    removed but fronds
    reserved, cut into
    thin wedges
200 g (7 oz) cherry
    tomatoes, halved
1 onion, finely sliced
3 garlic cloves, crushed
3 tablespoons olive oil, plus
    an extra drizzle to serve
200 ml (7 fl oz) vegan dry
    white wine
750 ml (1¼ pints) vegan stock
400 g (13 oz) pearl barley
3 thyme sprigs
50 g (2 oz) Kalamata olives,
    pitted and halved
salt and pepper

Preheat the oven to 190°C (375°F), Gas Mark 5.

Toss together the fennel, tomatoes, onion, garlic, olive oil and some salt and pepper in a large, deep roasting tray. Roast for 20–30 minutes until the fennel and onion are lightly golden.

Remove the tray from the oven, add the wine, stock, pearl barley and thyme and stir to combine, then return to the oven for another 30 minutes, or until the pearl barley is cooked but with a slight bite to it and the fennel is tender. If it is too dry, add a little more stock.

Roughly chop the fennel fronds, then stir through the barley mixture along with the olives, and finish with a drizzle of olive oil before serving.

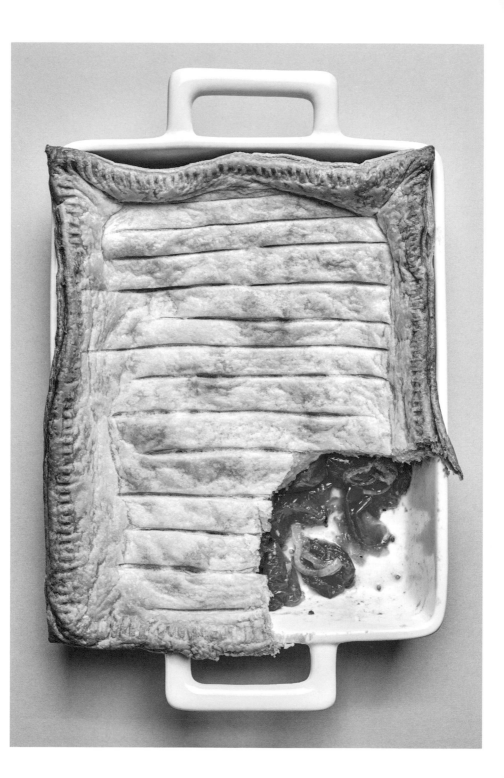

ROASTED TOMATO & ONION PUFF PIE

A really simple and flavourful pie, with a filling of sweet and unctuous tomatoes flavoured with garlic and oregano and a crispy, flaky pastry top. The squash and sage filling makes an ideal autumn or winter option (see below).

SERVES 4

1 kg (2 lb) mixed ripe tomatoes, such as plum and cherry, halved or cut into chunks, depending on size

3 onions, finely sliced

4 garlic cloves, crushed

leaves from 3 oregano sprigs, roughly chopped

3 tablespoons olive oil

320 g (11 oz) sheet ready-rolled vegan puff pastry

salt and pepper

Preheat the oven to 190°C (375°F), Gas Mark 5.

Toss together the tomatoes, onions, garlic, oregano, olive oil and a generous pinch of salt and pepper in a pie dish or roasting tray about 20 x 30 cm (8 x 12 inches). Roast for 30 minutes until the tomatoes are starting to burst and colour.

Lay the puff pastry sheet over the top, press on to the dish or tray edges and trim off any excess. Press around the pastry edges with the tines of a fork to seal. Feel free to make a random pattern with the trimmings and arrange on top of the pastry. Pierce a hole in the centre of the pastry lid with the tip of a knife to allow the steam to escape and bake for 30 minutes until the pastry is golden brown.

FOR ROASTED SQUASH & SAGE PUFF PIE, swap the tomatoes for 1 butternut squash (about 1 kg/2 lb), peeled, deseeded and cut into 1 cm (½ inch) thick slices, and the oregano for 6 sage leaves, roughly chopped.

ROAST CAULIFLOWER BAKE

This is like a fancy cauliflower cheese but with a velvety soft sauce made from some of the cauliflower, flavoured with roasted garlic, tahini and lemon.

SERVES 2

50 g (2 oz) blanched
hazelnuts
1 large cauliflower
6 garlic cloves, unpeeled
olive oil
finely grated zest and juice
of 1 lemon
2 tablespoons tahini
50 ml (2 fl oz) oat milk
salt and pepper

To serve
handful of parsley leaves
pinch of chilli flakes

Preheat the oven to 190°C (375°F), Gas Mark 5.

Spread the hazelnuts out in a deep roasting tray and roast for about 10 minutes until golden brown.

Meanwhile, cut the stalk off the cauliflower, then trim and cut it into pieces or slices. Discard any scraggly outer leaves but cut off the rest and reserve. Cut the head of the cauliflower into medium-sized florets.

Transfer the roasted hazelnuts to a chopping board and leave to cool. Put all the cauliflower into the roasting tray along with the garlic cloves, drizzle with olive oil and season with salt and pepper. Roast for about 30 minutes until the cauliflower is starting to colour and is tender enough to stick a fork into easily.

Take the tray out of the oven and remove half of the cauliflower, mainly the stalk pieces, leaving the best-looking florets in the tray, and put into a blender. Squeeze the soft roasted garlic out of the skins into the blender and add the lemon zest and juice, tahini and oat milk. Blitz until you have a smooth and silky purée. Taste and add salt and pepper if needed.

Dollop the purée back into the tray and swirl it gently into the cauliflower florets, then return to the oven for another 10 minutes.

Meanwhile, roughly chop the hazelnuts.

Serve the cauliflower bake sprinkled with the hazelnuts along with the parsley leaves and chilli flakes.

LENTIL & MUSHROOM PIE

A creamy, saucy ragout of lentils and mushrooms is perfectly contrasted by a topping of grated root vegetables (which can easily be varied – see below), baked until crisp and golden brown. This dish is a real plonk-in-the-middle-of-the-table-and-get-stuck-in kind of meal.

SERVES 6

2 tablespoons olive oil

2 onions, finely chopped

2 carrots, peeled and finely chopped

2 celery sticks, finely chopped

3 garlic cloves, crushed

250 g (8 oz) chestnut mushrooms, roughly chopped

1 tablespoon fennel seeds

2 tablespoons vegan red wine vinegar

2 x 400 g (13 oz) cans green lentils, drained and rinsed

2 tablespoons wholegrain mustard

2 tablespoons plain flour

400 ml (14 fl oz) vegan stock

salt and pepper

Celeriac & sweet potato topping

½ celeriac (about 500 g/1 lb), peeled and grated

250 g (8 oz) sweet potatoes, peeled and grated

1 teaspoon dried thyme

drizzle of olive oil

pinch of salt and pepper

Preheat the oven to 190°C (375°F), Gas Mark 5.

Heat the olive oil in a shallow ovenproof casserole dish, add the onions, carrots and celery with the garlic and cook over a medium heat for about 8 minutes until soft.

Add the mushrooms, fennel seeds and vinegar and cook for another 5 minutes.

Mix in the lentils and mustard, then stir in the flour, ensuring there are no lumps, and cook for a minute or so. Pour over the stock, bring to a simmer, stirring, and cook for 10 minutes until thickened. Season with salt and pepper to taste.

Take off the heat and leave to stand while you mix together all the topping ingredients in a bowl.

Cover the lentil mixture with the topping mixture in an even layer and bake for about 40 minutes until golden brown.

FOR POTATO, CARROT & BEETROOT TOPPING, swap the celeriac and sweet potato for 2 medium white potatoes, 2 carrots and 1 large beetroot, all peeled and grated, and use 1 teaspoon fennel seeds instead of the dried thyme.

ROASTED SQUASH & KALE WITH HERBY YOGURT DRESSING

This warm salad of autumnal or wintry squash is lightened by a creamy fresh herb dressing, with some crunchy toasted pumpkin seeds added for texture. Delicious!

SERVES 4

50 g (2 oz) pumpkin seeds
1 butternut squash (about
    1 kg/2 lb), deseeded and
    cut into 2 cm (¾ inch)
    thick wedges
2 tablespoons olive oil
2 garlic cloves, crushed
1 teaspoon paprika
pinch of chilli flakes
2 tablespoons maple syrup
150 g (5 oz) kale, ribs
    removed and large leaves
    torn into smaller pieces
salt and pepper

Herby yogurt dressing
200 g (7 oz) soya or other
    dairy-free yogurt
leaves from 20 g (¾ oz)
    coriander sprigs
leaves from 20 g (¾ oz)
    mint sprigs
salt and pepper

Preheat the oven to 200°C (400°F), Gas Mark 6.

Spread the pumpkin seeds out in a large ovenproof dish and roast for 12 minutes. Transfer the roasted pumpkin seeds to a chopping board and leave to cool.

Toss the squash wedges with the olive oil, garlic, paprika, chilli flakes, maple syrup and a large pinch of salt and pepper in the ovenproof dish, then roast for about 30–40 minutes until soft, golden and slightly crispy around the edges. About 10 minutes before the squash is ready, add the kale, tossing it through the squash with a little more olive oil if needed and tucking the leaves snugly under the squash pieces.

Meanwhile, make the herby yogurt dressing. Put the yogurt, coriander and mint leaves and a pinch of salt and pepper in a blender and blitz together until you have a smooth, pale green sauce.

Serve the roasted pumpkin and kale drizzled with the herby yogurt dressing and scattered with the roasted pumpkin seeds.

POTATO & DILL QUICK PIZZA

The inspiration for this dish is German pizza, which doesn't involve making a yeast bread dough or a sauce. Just roll out your dough, spread over the vegan crème fraîche and top with whatever vegetables you fancy, as long as they can be cooked quickly. Here, the potatoes are grated so they cook through in time.

SERVES 2-4

Dough
250 g (8 oz) plain flour, plus extra for dusting
½ teaspoon baking powder
½ teaspoon salt
3 tablespoons olive oil, plus extra for greasing
100 ml (3½ fl oz) warm water

Potato & dill topping
300 g (10 oz) potatoes, peeled and grated
1 shallot, thinly sliced
olive oil
150 g (5 oz) vegan crème fraîche
3 tablespoons roughly chopped dill fronds
salt and pepper

Preheat the grill to a medium-high heat and grease a large baking tray with olive oil.

Mix together the dough ingredients in a large bowl until the mixture comes together into a dough. Knead the dough on a lightly floured work top for a few minutes.

Put the dough back in the bowl, cover, and allow to sit for 30 minutes. Then roll out into a thin rectangle and transfer to the greased baking tray. Grill for 5–7 minutes until golden.

Meanwhile, wrap the potato and shallot in a clean tea towel and squeeze out all the excess moisture. Drizzle olive oil over the potato and shallot, season, and mix together.

Flip the grilled dough over and spread a layer of the vegan crème fraîche on the pizza base. Evenly scatter over the potato and shallot mixture and grill for a further 6–10 minutes until the pizza is golden and the potato is crispy on top. Sprinkle over the dill, cut into wedges and serve.

FOR ARTICHOKE & COURGETTE QUICK PIZZA, cook the dough as above, but swap the potatoes, shallot and dill for 200 g (7 oz) shop-bought chargrilled artichokes and 100 g (3½ oz) thinly sliced courgettes. Arrange in a single layer over the vegan crème fraîche, drizzle with olive oil and season. Grill for a further 6–10 minutes until golden.

FOR RED ONION & OLIVE QUICK PIZZA, cook the dough as above, but swap the potatoes, shallot and dill for 1 thinly sliced red onion and 100 g (3½ oz) olives, pitted and halved. Arrange in a single layer over the vegan crème fraîche, drizzle with olive oil and season. Grill for a further 6–10 minutes until golden.

SWEET & SOUR CRISPY TOFU

A fail-safe recipe with all the flavours of the takeaway classic. If you don't fancy tofu or would like to try something a bit different, use aubergines instead (see below), or courgettes or cauliflower.

SERVES 4

300 g (10 oz) block firm tofu
2 tablespoons light soy sauce
¼ teaspoon salt
¼ teaspoon ground black
  pepper
3 tablespoons cornflour
100 ml (3½ fl oz)
  vegetable oil
1 red pepper, sliced
1 green pepper, sliced
1 onion, finely sliced
4 garlic cloves, crushed
2.5 cm (1 inch) piece of
  ginger, peeled and grated
100 g (3½ oz) baby corn, cut
  into 2 cm (¾ inch) chunks
100 g (3½ oz) canned,
  drained sliced bamboo
  shoots
4 tablespoons apple cider
  vinegar
2 tablespoons light brown
  sugar
2 tablespoons tomato purée
400 ml (14 fl oz) vegan stock
200 g (7 oz) rice vermicelli
  noodles
3 spring onions, finely sliced
  on the diagonal, to serve

Wrap the tofu in a clean tea towel and weigh it down with a heavy chopping board or cookbook for 1 hour, then remove and cut into 2.5 cm (1 inch) chunks.

Toss the tofu with the soy sauce in a bowl, then add the salt, pepper and cornflour and toss until evenly coated.

Heat the oil in a large wok or frying pan over a medium heat. Add the tofu in batches and fry for 3–5 minutes until crisp and golden brown. Remove with a slotted spoon and drain on a plate lined with kitchen paper.

Carefully pour off some of the oil, if necessary, to leave about 3 tablespoons in the pan and increase the heat slightly. Add the peppers and onion and fry for about 5–8 minutes until softened. Then add the garlic, ginger, baby corn and bamboo shoots and stir-fry for 2 minutes.

Add the vinegar, sugar, tomato purée and stock and cook, stirring, until the sugar has dissolved. Stir in the tofu and cook for another 2 minutes, or until the sauce thickens.

Meanwhile, quickly rinse out the tofu bowl, add the rice noodles and pour over boiling water to cover, then leave for about 1 minute until softened.

Drain the noodles, add to the pan and toss with the sauce and tofu for a minute or so. Serve topped with the spring onions.

FOR SWEET & SOUR CRISPY AUBERGINE, swap the tofu for 3 aubergines, cut into 2 cm (¾ inch) cubes. Sprinkle with salt and leave for 2 minutes, then pat dry with kitchen paper before preparing in the same way as the tofu, to ensure a crispier result when fried. Cook and serve as above.

LEEK & FENNEL BREAD PUDDING

A genius way to use up old bread, along with any spare vegetables that may be lurking in your refrigerator, this bread pudding is creamy, savoury and so simple to put together.

SERVES 4–6

2 tablespoons olive oil

2 leeks, thoroughly washed, halved lengthways and cut into thin half-moons

1 fennel bulb, any tough outer layers and stalks removed, finely sliced

3 garlic cloves, crushed

1 tablespoon roughly chopped rosemary leaves

1 teaspoon cornflour

400 g (13 oz) lightly toasted sourdough bread, ripped into smallish chunks

750 ml (1¼ pints) oat milk

salt and pepper

Preheat the oven to 200°C (400°F), Gas Mark 6.

Heat the olive oil in a shallow ovenproof casserole dish, add the leeks and cook for 5 minutes until softened. Then add the fennel, garlic and rosemary and cook for another 5 minutes. Stir in the cornflour until all the ingredients are lightly coated.

Add the sourdough chunks, season with salt and pepper and pour over the oat milk, then gently stir to combine. Bake for 30 minutes.

Leave the pudding to cool for 10 minutes before serving.

FOR TOMATO & OLIVE BREAD PUDDING, prepare and cook the pudding as above, but swap the leeks for 1 finely sliced onion, softening it in just 1 tablespoon olive oil. Then replace the fennel and rosemary with 500 g (1 lb) cherry tomatoes, halved, and 75 g (3 oz) Kalamata olives, pitted, cooking them along with the garlic. Scatter a handful of basil leaves, torn, over the baked and slightly cooled pudding before serving.

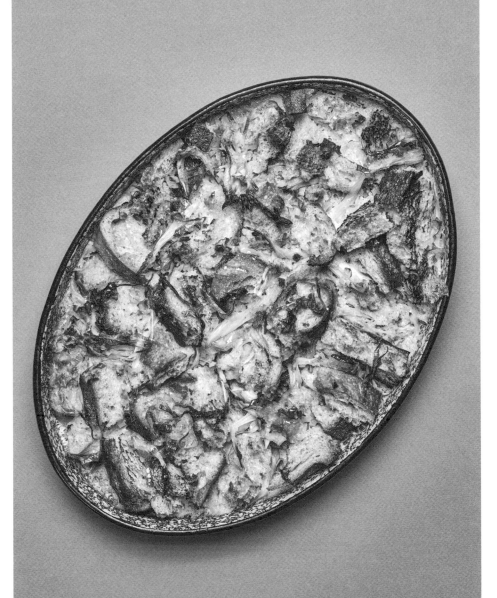

TAHINI AUBERGINE COUSCOUS WITH DUKKAH

The dukkah, a spice and nut mix originally from Egypt, can be used to season many different dishes, such as sprinkled over avocado on toast or the Aromatic Chickpea Stew (see page 59). It will keep for several weeks in a tightly sealed jar.

SERVES 4

2 large aubergines
4 garlic cloves, unpeeled
3 tablespoons olive oil
1 tablespoon ground sumac
200 g (7 oz) couscous
300 ml (10 fl oz) hot
    vegan stock
100 g (3½ oz) tahini
1 tablespoon lemon juice
1 tablespoon maple syrup
2 tablespoons water
handful of mint leaves,
    roughly chopped
handful of parsley leaves,
    roughly chopped
75 g (3 oz) pomegranate
    seeds
salt and pepper

Dukkah
100 g (3½ oz) almonds or
    walnuts
1 tablespoon coriander seeds
1 tablespoon cumin seeds
1 tablespoon fennel seeds
1 teaspoon salt

Preheat the oven to 200°C (400°F), Gas Mark 6.

First make the dukkah. Heat a large, shallow ovenproof dish over a medium heat, add the nuts and gently toast for about 6–8 minutes, stirring, until lightly coloured all over. Add all the spice seeds and toast for 2–3 minutes until their aromas are released.

Lightly crush the mix using a pestle and mortar. Alternatively, tip into a jar and crush with the back of a spoon. Stir through the salt and set aside.

Halve the aubergines lengthways, then lightly score the cut side and sprinkle with salt. Put the aubergine halves in the casserole dish and tuck the garlic cloves underneath. Drizzle with olive oil, sprinkle over the sumac and season with salt and pepper. Roast in the oven for 20–30 minutes until soft and crispy.

Take the dish out of the oven and turn it off. Move the aubergines to one side of the dish, then use the back of a spoon to squeeze the soft roasted garlic out of the skins, discarding the skins. Add the couscous and hot stock and stir to combine. Arrange the aubergines on top of the couscous and return to the still-hot oven for 10 minutes until the couscous has absorbed the stock.

Meanwhile, whisk together the tahini, lemon juice, maple syrup, measured water and a pinch of salt and pepper in a bowl. Drizzle the tahini dressing over the couscous, then scatter over the herbs, pomegranate seeds and a few tablespoons of the dukkah before serving.

SIMPLE SWEETS

APPLE & MARZIPAN GALETTE

A rustic apple tart made sweet and easy with shop-bought marzipan rather than a homemade frangipane. You don't even need to peel the apples!

SERVES 6–8

4 apples, cored and cut into
  1 cm (½ inch) thick slices
50 g (2 oz) caster sugar, plus
  extra for sprinkling over
  the pastry
1 tablespoon vanilla extract
juice of ½ lemon
200 g (7 oz) vegan marzipan,
  broken into smallish chunks

Pastry
125 g (4 oz) plain flour, plus
  extra for dusting
65 g (2½ oz) cold vegan
  butter, cut into small cubes
20 g (¾ oz) icing sugar
¼ teaspoon salt
2 tablespoons cold water
2 tablespoons almond milk
  or other dairy-free milk, for
  brushing the pastry

First make the pastry. Put the flour in a bowl, add the vegan butter and rub in with your fingertips until the mixture resembles coarse breadcrumbs (you want the butter to be as cold as possible, so try not to handle it too much). Stir in the icing sugar and salt.

Mix in the measured cold water until the mixture starts to form clumps, then bring it together with your hands and briefly knead into a smooth ball of dough. Wrap in clingfilm or a reusable beeswax food wrap and chill in the refrigerator for 20 minutes, or until ready to use.

Meanwhile, preheat the oven to 200°C (400°F), Gas Mark 6. Line a large baking tray with nonstick baking paper.

Rinse out the pastry bowl, add the apples, sugar, vanilla and lemon juice and mix until the apples are evenly coated.

Roll out the pastry on a lightly floured work top into a 35 cm (13¾ inch) circle about 2.5 mm (⅛ inch) thick and transfer to the lined baking tray.

Spread out the marzipan chunks evenly over the pastry circle, leaving a 5 cm (2 inch) border around the edge. Pile the apple slices on to the marzipan and then fold the pastry edge over the apples so that the filling is firmly contained.

Brush the pastry with the almond or other dairy-free milk and sprinkle with extra sugar to give the pastry a sweet crunch. Bake for 40–50 minutes until the pastry is golden brown and the apples are soft and caramelized.

Leave the galette to cool for 10 minutes before cutting into slices and serving.

SAUCY CHOCOLATE PUDDING

For a minimal-effort dessert with maximum results, try this rich and gooey chocolate pudding with its own sauce built in. Or use the same basic method to make two other flavour variations (see below).

SERVES 8

Chocolate pudding
150 g (5 oz) caster sugar
75 g (3 oz) plain flour
30 g (1 oz) ground almonds
75 g (3 oz) cocoa powder
½ teaspoon baking powder
¼ teaspoon salt
100 ml (3½ fl oz) preferably
   almond milk or other
   dairy-free milk
1 teaspoon vanilla extract
75 ml (3 fl oz) vegetable oil,
   plus extra for greasing

Chocolate sauce
100 g (3½ oz) caster sugar
50 g (2 oz) light brown sugar
40 g (1½ oz) cocoa powder
½ teaspoon vanilla extract
¼ teaspoon salt
350 ml (12 fl oz) boiling
   water

Preheat the oven to 180°C (350°F), Gas Mark 4. Grease a medium-sized ovenproof dish about 20–23cm (8–9 inches) in diameter and at least 7 cm (3 inches) deep with a little vegetable oil.

Whisk together all the pudding ingredients in a bowl, then spread out the batter evenly in the greased dish.

Mix together the sugars, cocoa powder, vanilla and salt for the sauce in the same bowl, then carefully spread the mixture over the pudding batter. Pour over the measured boiling water and bake straight away for 35–40 minutes.

Leave the pudding to cool for 10 minutes before serving.

FOR SAUCY TOFFEE PUDDING, put 150 g (5 oz) pitted and finely chopped dates in a bowl with ⅛ teaspoon bicarbonate of soda. Pour over 75 ml (3 fl oz) boiling water and leave to soak for 20 minutes. Then add the pudding ingredients as above but only 50 ml (2 fl oz) dairy-free milk. Whisk together as before. For the sauce, swap the caster sugar, light brown sugar and cocoa for 150 g (5 oz) dark brown sugar. Dot 25 g (1 oz) vegan butter in small pieces over the top of the sugar mixture before pouring over the boiling water and baking as above.

FOR SAUCY LEMON PUDDING, swap the cocoa powder in the batter for the zest of 3 lemons and the juice of 1, and use 115 g (3¾ oz) plain flour. For the sauce, use 150 g (5 oz) caster sugar (omitting the brown sugar, cocoa powder, salt and vanilla) and dot 25 g (1 oz) vegan butter in small pieces over the top of the pudding batter. Mix 1½ tablespoons cornflour with the juice of the 2 remaining lemons until smooth. Stir in the boiling water and pour over the sugar-sprinkled pudding batter. Bake as above.

NECTARINE & RASPBERRY COBBLER

A cobbler is such a great way to enjoy, in essence, scones and jam. Here, a balance of sweet and tart roasted fruits marries perfectly with the soft cakey topping and its sugared crunch.

SERVES 6–8

750 g (1½ lb) ripe nectarines, pitted and cut into eighths
100 g (3½ oz) caster sugar
1 teaspoon vanilla extract
finely grated zest and juice of 1 lemon
250 g (8 oz) raspberries

Cobbler topping
240 g (7¾ oz) plain flour
2 teaspoons baking powder
75 g (3 oz) caster sugar, plus extra for sprinkling
finely grated zest of 1 lemon
125 g (4 oz) cold vegan butter, cut into small cubes
200 ml (7 fl oz) oat or soya milk

Preheat the oven to 200°C (400°F), Gas Mark 6.

Toss the nectarines with the sugar, vanilla and lemon zest and juice in an ovenproof dish about 20 x 30 cm (8 x 12 inches). Roast for 15 minutes.

Take the dish out of the oven and stir through the raspberries, then set aside while you make the cobbler topping.

Mix together the flour, baking powder, sugar and lemon zest in a bowl. Add the vegan butter and rub in with your fingertips until the mixture resembles coarse breadcrumbs. Mix in the oat or soya milk until the mixture just starts to come together.

Dollop heaped tablespoons of the cobbler batter on top of the fruit with a little space in between, then sprinkle with sugar.

Bake for about 20 minutes until the cobbler topping is golden brown and the fruit is soft. Leave to cool for 5 minutes or so before serving.

FOR RHUBARB & STRAWBERRY COBBLER, swap the nectarines and raspberries for 750 g (1½ lb) trimmed rhubarb, cut into 4 cm (1½ inch) lengths (and halved lengthways if the rhubarb is particularly thick), and 300 g (10 oz) strawberries, hulled and quartered, and use orange zest and juice instead of lemon. Bake and serve as above.

MINT CHOCOLATE AQUAFABA MOUSSE

If you love mint chocolate, this is the dessert for you. But even if mint flavouring isn't to your liking, you can simply omit the peppermint extract entirely, or swap it for orange extract for an equally delicious result.

SERVES 4–6

150 g (5 oz) vegan dark chocolate, broken into small chunks

175 ml (6 fl oz) canned chickpea liquid (aquafaba), drained from a 400 g (13 oz) can chickpeas (reserve the chickpeas for use in another recipe)

pinch of salt

½ teaspoon vegan white wine vinegar

100 g (3½ oz) caster sugar

¾ teaspoon peppermint extract

Candied mint decoration (optional)

a few springs of fresh mint leaves

2 tablespoons aquafaba

3 tablespoons caster sugar

Put the chocolate in a microwave-proof bowl and heat in a microwave on low in 30-second bursts, stirring after each burst, until the chocolate is completely melted (be careful, as it can burn quite easily) Alternatively, melt the chocolate in a heatproof bowl set over a pan of barely simmering water. Set aside until completely cool but still runny.

Put the aquafaba in the bowl of a stand mixer or a clean bowl and whisk with the mixer or an electric hand whisk on high speed for 5 minutes until opaque and stiff.

Add the salt and vinegar and, while whisking slowly, add the sugar one tablespoon at a time. Gently whisk in the peppermint extract, then carefully fold in the cooled melted chocolate until well combined.

Pour the mixture back into the chocolate bowl (no need to wash!) and chill in the refrigerator for 1 hour, or until ready to serve.

Meanwhile, prepare the decoration. Brush the mint leaves very lightly with aquafaba and dip in the caster sugar before placing on top of the set mousse.

Serve the mousse in large spoonfuls.

BAKEWELL PUDDING

A recipe that pays homage to the classic British Bakewell tart, with a layer of zesty cherries and a soft, sweet and almondy topping. If you prefer something a little tarter, try using apricots, which work so well with the frangipane (see below).

SERVES 6

vegetable oil or vegan butter,
  for greasing
500 g (1 lb) frozen cherries
50 g (2 oz) caster sugar
finely grated zest of 1 orange
  and 1 tablespoon juice
1 tablespoon vanilla extract

Frangipane
150 g (5 oz) vegan butter,
  softened
175 g (6 oz) caster sugar
200 g (7 oz) ground almonds
50 g (2 oz) plain flour
½ teaspoon baking powder
125 ml (4 fl oz) almond milk
1 teaspoon almond extract
1 tablespoon kirsch (optional)
50 g (2 oz) flaked almonds

Preheat the oven to 180°C (350°F), Gas Mark 4. Grease a deep ovenproof dish about 16 x 23 cm (6¼ x 9 inches) with vegetable oil or vegan butter.

Toss the cherries with the sugar, orange zest and juice and vanilla in the dish and bake for 15 minutes.

Meanwhile, put the vegan butter and sugar for the frangipane in a bowl and beat with an electric hand whisk until pale and fluffy.

Mix in the ground almonds, flour and baking powder, then slowly add the almond milk and extract, and kirsch if using, until you have a smooth batter.

Take the dish out of the oven and dollop the frangipane batter evenly over the cherries. Scatter over the flaked almonds and bake for about 45 minutes until the frangipane is fairly firm and golden.

FOR APRICOT FRANGIPANE PUDDING, swap the cherries for 500 g (1 lb) apricots, pitted and quartered, and toss with 100 g (3½ oz) caster sugar and only 1 teaspoon vanilla extract, omitting the orange zest and juice. Omit the kirsch from the frangipane batter. Bake and serve as above.

DROP DOUGHNUTS

These quick and easy doughnuts are made from a simple batter that doesn't require yeast, so it is just a case of whisking the ingredients together and dropping the batter into the hot oil. They are best eaten on the day, which won't prove too much of a challenge!

SERVES 6

350 g (11½ oz) plain flour
65 g (2½ oz) caster sugar
1 tablespoon baking powder
½ teaspoon salt
250 ml (8 fl oz) oat milk
finely grated zest of 2 oranges
3 tablespoons vegetable oil,
    plus 750 ml (1¼ pints)
    for frying
1 heaped tablespoon
    shop-bought apple sauce
    or apple purée
1 teaspoon vanilla extract

Cinnamon sugar
100 g (3½ oz) caster sugar
1 teaspoon ground cinnamon

Mix together all the dry ingredients in a large bowl, then make a well in the centre. Whisk together all the wet ingredients, except the vegetable oil for frying, in a jug, pour into the well and gradually whisk in the dry ingredients until you have a thick smooth batter.

Heat the vegetable oil for frying in a medium-sized, deep saucepan over a medium heat, ensuring there is at least 5 cm (2 inches) between the surface of the oil and the top of the pan to avoid the hot oil bubbling over.

Meanwhile, line a plate with kitchen paper and have a heatproof slotted spoon ready.

Mix together the sugar and cinnamon in a shallow bowl.

Check the temperature of the oil by gently dropping a tiny bit of the batter into the oil – if it is hot enough, it will start to sizzle.

Dollop heaped tablespoons of the doughnut batter into the hot oil in batches of 4 and fry for 2 minutes on each side until golden brown. If the doughnuts are overbrowning, reduce the heat slightly.

Remove the cooked doughnuts with the slotted spoon and drain on the kitchen paper. When cool enough to handle, roll in the cinnamon sugar and serve

FOR BANANA DROP DOUGHNUTS, add 3 ripe bananas, peeled and mashed, with the other wet ingredients but omit the orange zest and use only 175 ml (6 fl oz) oat milk. Dust the fried doughnuts with icing sugar rather than cinnamon sugar, if you like.

BAKED PUMPKIN PUDDING

A lightly spiced custard-like pumpkin pudding, this is basically pumpkin pie without the pastry. It is made with shop-bought pumpkin purée, which you can find in most supermarkets and will save you loads of time – and cleaning up!

SERVES 6

425 g (14 oz) can pumpkin
  purée
225 ml (7½ fl oz) almond milk
  or other dairy-free milk
125 g (4 oz) light brown
  sugar
3 tablespoons cornflour
¾ teaspoon ground
  cinnamon
¼ teaspoon ground ginger
a few gratings of nutmeg
1 teaspoon vanilla extract

Preheat the oven to 180°C (350°F), Gas Mark 4.

Whisk together all the ingredients in a bowl until well combined.

Pour the mixture into a medium-sized, shallow ovenproof dish and bake for about 40 minutes until set in the centre.

Take the pudding out of the oven and leave it to cool for 10 minutes before serving. Alternatively, leave to cool completely and then chill in the refrigerator for 1 hour if you want to enjoy it cold.

COCONUT STICKY RICE WITH GINGER & MANGO

This recipe is inspired by Thai sweet sticky rice and kiribath, Sri Lankan coconut milk rice. There is something infinitely comforting about eating a soft block of sweet coconut sticky rice.

SERVES 4

200 g (7 oz) jasmine rice or glutinous (sticky) rice, washed and drained
½ teaspoon salt
300 ml (½ pint) water
400 ml (14 fl oz) can coconut milk
100 g (3½ oz) caster sugar
40 g (1½ oz) crystallized stem ginger, roughly chopped

To serve
2 mangoes, peeled, pitted and thinly sliced
1 tablespoon black sesame seeds (optional)

Put the rice and salt in a medium-sized saucepan, pour over the measured water and bring to a gentle simmer, stirring.

Cook, stirring frequently, for 20 minutes until the rice is soft and the water has been absorbed.

Stir in the remaining ingredients and cook for another 20 minutes until the rice is thick and creamy, stirring occasionally.

Lay a piece of nonstick baking paper on a work top and spread the rice mixture over it in an even layer about 2.5 cm (1 inch) thick. Cover with another piece of nonstick baking paper and leave to cool completely.

Either chill in the refrigerator before serving or serve at room temperature. Cut into small rectangles and serve with the mango, sprinkled with the black sesame seeds if you like.

FOR COCONUT STICKY RICE WITH ROSE & PISTACHIO, swap the ginger for 1 teaspoon rosewater. When ready to serve, scatter over 50 g (2 oz) pistachio nuts, roughly chopped, along with 1 tablespoon dried rose petals if you like.

PEANUT BUTTER SKILLET COOKIE

An ooey gooey cookie and dessert in one – what more could anyone want? Particularly delicious with vegan ice cream. The dough can also be baked as individual cookies for when you need or fancy something more portable – simply roll into walnut-sized balls and bake on a baking tray lined with nonstick baking paper for 18 minutes. If you don't like or can't eat peanut butter, or if you just want an extra-chocolaty cookie, try the double chocolate option (see below).

SERVES 8

100 g (3½ oz) vegan butter, softened, plus extra for greasing
100 g (3½ oz) smooth peanut butter
150 g (5 oz) light brown sugar
100 g (3½ oz) caster sugar
2 teaspoons vanilla extract
2 heaped tablespoons shop-bought apple sauce or apple purée
250 g (8 oz) plain flour
1 teaspoon bicarbonate of soda
½ teaspoon salt
125 g (4 oz) vegan dark chocolate, chopped into smallish chunks

Preheat the oven to 180°C (350°F), Gas Mark 4. Grease an ovenproof skillet or pie dish about 23 cm (9 inches) in diameter with vegan butter.

Put the vegan butter, peanut butter, sugars and vanilla in a large bowl and beat together until pale and creamy.

Mix in the apple sauce or purée, then sift over the flour, bicarbonate of soda and salt and gently fold in. Stir in the chocolate chunks.

Dollop the cookie dough on to the greased skillet or dish, then spread it over the base. Bake for 25–30 minutes, or until the cookie is still slightly gooey in the centre but crisp around the edge.

Cut into wedges, or simply scoop out and serve. Any leftovers can be stored in an airtight container after baking for 5 days.

FOR DOUBLE CHOCOLATE SKILLET COOKIE, make the cookie dough as above but use 200 g (7 oz) vegan butter instead of half vegan butter and half peanut butter and 200 g (7 oz) plain flour and 50 g (2 oz) cocoa powder, sifted together, rather than 250 g plain flour. Bake and serve as above.

SWEET BUNS 3 WAYS

These sweet pillows are wonderfully soft. The buns take a bit of extra time to make, as the dough is yeasted, but it is totally worth the effort. And it is easy to vary the filling and glaze for a range of flavour options.

COCONUT MILK SCROLLS

MAKES 12

Sweet bun dough
660 g (1 lb 6 oz) strong white flour, plus extra for dusting
125 g (4 oz) coconut oil or vegan butter, softened, plus extra for greasing
75 g (3 oz) caster sugar
7 g sachet (2¼ teaspoons) fast-action dried yeast
½ teaspoon ground nutmeg
½ teaspoon salt
400 ml (14 fl oz) can coconut milk

Coconut & vanilla filling
100 ml (3½ fl oz) coconut milk
150 g (5 oz) desiccated coconut
75 g (3 oz) caster sugar
1 teaspoon vanilla extract
¼ teaspoon salt

Coconut glaze
100 g (3½ oz) icing sugar
3 tablespoons coconut milk

Put all the dough ingredients in a large bowl and mix until it forms a dough. Knead the dough on a lightly floured work top for 10 minutes until smooth.

Lightly dust the inside of the mixing bowl with flour, then return the dough and cover with a clean tea towel. Leave to prove in a warm place for 1 hour, or until doubled in size.

Meanwhile, mix together the filling ingredients in a bowl until well combined and grease a large baking tray with a little coconut oil or vegan butter and line with nonstick baking paper.

When the dough has risen, press down on it firmly to deflate it and then roll out on a lightly floured work top into a rectangle about 30 x 40 cm (12 x 16 inches).

Spread the filling evenly over the dough, leaving a 2 cm (¾ inch) border around the edges. Starting from one of the longer sides of the rectangle, roll up the pastry as tightly as possible until you have a long roll.

Cut the roll into 12 even slices and slightly space them out on the prepared baking tray. Cover with the tea towel and leave to prove for 30 minutes.

Meanwhile, preheat the oven to 200°C (400°F), Gas Mark 6.

Bake the scrolls for 25–30 minutes until golden brown and springy to touch. Leave to cool slightly. Mix together the glaze ingredients in a bowl and then drizzle over the still-warm buns. These are best eaten on the day of baking.

CINNAMON SCROLLS

1 quantity Sweet Bun Dough
  (see page 129)

Cinnamon filling
100 g (3½ oz) light brown
  sugar
2 tablespoons ground
  cinnamon
50 g (2 oz) coconut oil or
  vegan butter, melted

Maple glaze
100 g (3½ oz) icing sugar
2 tablespoons maple syrup

Roll out the proved and deflated dough into a rectangle as for the Coconut Milk Scrolls (see page 129).

Mix together the sugar and cinnamon for the filling. Spread the coconut oil or vegan butter evenly over the dough, leaving a 2 cm (¾ inch) border, then sprinkle evenly with the cinnamon sugar. Roll up, slice, prove and then bake as on page 129.

Combine the glaze ingredients, drizzle over the still-warm buns and serve.

DARK CHOCOLATE & HAZELNUT SCROLLS

1 quantity Sweet Bun Dough
  (see page 129)

Chocolate & hazelnut filling
50 g (2 oz) vegan dark
  chocolate, finely chopped
50 g (2 oz) blanched
  hazelnuts, roasted (see
  page 94) and finely
  chopped
2 tablespoons light brown
  sugar
50 g (2 oz) coconut oil or
  vegan butter, melted

Icing glaze
200 g (7 oz) icing sugar
about 3 tablespoons water

Roll out the proved and deflated dough into a rectangle as for the Coconut Milk Scrolls (see page 129).

Mix together the chocolate, hazelnuts and sugar for the filling. Spread the coconut oil or vegan butter evenly over the dough, leaving a 2 cm (¾ inch) border, then sprinkle evenly with the chocolate and nut mixture. Roll up, slice, prove and then bake as on page 129.

Combine the icing sugar with enough water to make a thinnish glaze and brush all over the still-warm buns.

APPLE & MINCEMEAT CRUMBLE SLAB PIE

This warmly spiced apple crumble pie is given a festive twist with the addition of mincemeat, though as this is usually on sale all year round, why not make it whenever you like. Alternatively, go for the apple and blackberry option (see page 132).

SERVES 8

Pastry
175 g (6 oz) plain flour
110 g (3¾ oz) cold vegan
   butter, cut into small
   cubes, plus extra for
   greasing
75 g (3 oz) ground almonds
60 g (2¼ oz) icing sugar
finely grated zest of 1 orange
pinch of salt
2 tablespoons cold water

Crumble
90 g (3¼ oz) cold vegan
   butter, cut into small cubes
50 g (2 oz) plain flour
75 g (3 oz) light brown sugar
50 g (2 oz) porridge oats
20 g (¾ oz) pecan nuts,
   roughly chopped
1 teaspoon ground cinnamon
pinch of salt

Filling
2 Granny Smith apples,
   peeled, cored and grated
500 g (1 lb) shop-bought
   vegan mincemeat

Preheat the oven to 190°C (375°F), Gas Mark 5. Grease a deep baking tray about 25 x 20 cm (10 x 8 inches) with a little vegan butter and line with nonstick baking paper.

First make the pastry. Put the flour in a large bowl, add the vegan butter and rub it in with your fingertips until the mixture resembles coarse breadcrumbs. Stir in the ground almonds, icing sugar, orange zest and salt.

Mix in the measured cold water until the mixture starts to form clumps, then bring it together with your hands and briefly knead into a smooth ball of dough.

Press the dough evenly over the base of the prepared tray and up the sides a little way. Prick it all over with a fork and bake for about 20 minutes until golden brown.

Meanwhile, using the same bowl, rub the vegan butter for the crumble into the flour as for the pastry.

Continued overleaf

Stir in the remaining crumble ingredients. Clump together some of the mixture to form large chunks, leaving the rest relatively fine in consistency.

Take the pastry out of the oven and leave to cool for 15 minutes. Then scatter over the grated apple and spread over the mincemeat in an even layer. Sprinkle over the crumble evenly and then bake for 40–45 minutes until the crumble is golden brown and the mincemeat mixture is bubbling through. Leave to cool for 10 minutes before slicing and serving.

FOR APPLE & BLACKBERRY CRUMBLE SLAB PIE, swap the mincemeat in the filling for 400 g (13 oz) blackberries and mix with the grated apple. Then sprinkle 2 tablespoons caster sugar over the fruit mixture after spreading it over the pastry and top with the crumble. Bake and serve as above.

CHOCOLATE GANACHE CAKE

A vegan take on a devil's food cake, this is an intensely chocolatey cake topped with dark chocolate ganache. It stays deliciously moist for a good few days.

SERVES 8

Cake

- 200 g (7 oz) plain flour
- 200 g (7 oz) caster sugar
- 100 g (3½ oz) light brown sugar
- 75 g (3 oz) cocoa powder
- 2 teaspoons bicarbonate of soda
- 1 teaspoon baking powder
- 1 teaspoon salt
- 400 ml (14 fl oz) can coconut milk, chilled and unshaken – use the liquid that has separated from the coconut cream (reserve the cream for the ganache) and top up it up with dairy-free milk to make 300 ml (10 fl oz)
- 125 ml (4 fl oz) vegetable oil, plus extra for greasing
- 1 tablespoon apple cider vinegar
- 1 teaspoon vanilla extract

Ganache

- 200 g (7 oz) thick coconut cream from the chilled can used for the cake (see left)
- 200 g (7 oz) vegan dark chocolate, chopped into smallish chunks
- pinch of salt

Preheat the oven to 180°C (350°C), Gas Mark 4. Grease a 23 cm (9 inch) round cake tin with a little vegetable oil and line with nonstick baking paper.

Mix together all the dry ingredients for the cake in a large bowl, then make a well in the centre. Whisk together the wet ingredients in a jug, pour into the well and gradually whisk in the dry ingredients from around the well, until only just combined but with no lumps.

Pour the cake batter into the prepared tin and bake for 45 minutes–1 hour until the cake is firm and springy to the touch, and a knife inserted into the centre comes out with only with a few crumbs on it. Leave the cake to cool completely while you make the ganache.

Mix the coconut cream with a pinch of salt in a microwave-proof bowl and heat in a microwave for 1½ minutes until it is melted and hot. Immediately add the chocolate and leave for 2 minutes before stirring until you have a glossy chocolate ganache. Leave to cool completely and thicken.

Spread the ganache over the cake and leave to set before cutting into slices. Keep in an airtight container for 5 days.

RASPBERRY & COCONUT MACAROON BARS

A dessert cake bar that has stood the test of time with its winning combination of a soft sponge bottom, a layer of sweet jam and a coconut macaroon-like topping.

MAKES 9

Sponge

125 g (4 oz) plain flour
75 g (3 oz) caster sugar
20 g (¾ oz) desiccated
    coconut
¾ teaspoon baking powder
¼ teaspoon fine salt
100 ml (3½ fl oz) dairy-free
    milk
75 ml (3 fl oz) coconut oil or
    vegetable oil, plus extra
    for greasing
½ tablespoon apple cider
    vinegar
1 teaspoon vanilla extract
200 g (7 oz) raspberry jam

Meringue

4 tablespoons canned
    chickpea liquid (aquafaba)
2 tablespoons caster sugar
100 g (3½ oz) desiccated
    coconut

Preheat the oven to 180°C (350°F), Gas Mark 4. Grease a 23 cm (9 inch) square cake tin with a little coconut oil or vegetable oil and line with nonstick baking paper.

Mix together all the dry ingredients for the sponge in a large bowl, then make a well in the centre. Whisk together all the wet ingredients, except the jam, in a jug, pour into the well and gradually whisk in the dry ingredients until only just combined but with no lumps.

Pour the sponge batter into the prepared tin and bake for about 15 minutes until the sponge is firm to the touch.

Leave the sponge to cool for 5 minutes, then spread over the jam and set aside while you make the meringue.

Whisk together the aquafaba and sugar with an electric hand whisk in a clean bowl until thick and foamy. Fold in the coconut.

Spread the meringue mixture evenly over the jam, then bake for about 20–30 minutes until the coconut is golden brown (cover the tin with foil if the coconut gets too brown before the cooking time is up).

Leave to cool for 30 minutes before slicing into 9 bars. These are best eaten on the day but can be kept in airtight container for up to 2 days.

FOR CHERRY MACAROON BARS, swap the raspberry jam for 400 g (13 oz) frozen cherries, halved and tossed with 2 tablespoons caster sugar and the finely grated zest of 1 lemon. Bake and serve as above.

LEMON DRIZZLE SEMOLINA CAKE

A light and easy vegan version of a great afternoon tea classic, this cake is seriously moist and zesty.

SERVES 8

Cake
200 g (7 oz) fine semolina
150 g (5 oz) caster sugar
½ teaspoon baking powder
½ teaspoon bicarbonate
    of soda
½ teaspoon salt
300 g (10 oz) soya yogurt
75 ml (3 fl oz) vegetable oil,
    plus extra for greasing
finely grated zest of 3 lemons
    and the juice of 1
1 teaspoon vanilla extract

Glaze
100 g (3½ oz) icing sugar
juice of 1 zested lemon used
    for the cake (see above)

Preheat the oven to 180°C (350°F), Gas Mark 4. Grease a 900 g (2 lb) loaf tin with a little vegetable oil and line with nonstick baking paper.

Mix together all the dry ingredients for the cake in a large bowl, then make a well in the centre. Whisk together all the wet ingredients in a jug, pour into the well and gradually whisk in the dry ingredients until only just combined but with no lumps.

Pour the cake batter into the prepared tin and bake for 20–25 minutes until the cake is firm to the touch. Leave to cool completely.

Wipe the mixing bowl clean, then add the icing sugar and lemon juice and whisk together to make a fairly thick glaze – if it is too thick and dry, add a little more water, and if too runny, add a little more icing sugar.

Spread the glaze evenly over the cake, allowing it to drip down the sides here and there. Leave to set if you are patient enough, otherwise eat straight away, storing any leftovers in an airtight container for up to 5 days.

PEAR & OLIVE OIL CAKE

A subtly sweet, fragrant and soft cake, you could almost eat this for breakfast.

SERVES 8

3 pears, cored and 2 sliced
125 ml (4 fl oz) olive oil, plus
    extra for greasing
75 ml (3 fl oz) dairy-free milk
finely grated zest of 1 lemon
1 teaspoon vanilla extract
250 g (8 oz) plain flour
125 g (4 oz) light brown
    sugar, plus 1 tablespoon
    for sprinkling
1 tablespoon baking powder
½ teaspoon salt

Preheat the oven to 180°C (350°F), Gas Mark 4. Grease a 20 cm (8 inch) round, preferably springform, cake tin with a little olive oil and line with nonstick baking paper.

Put the unsliced pear in a jug and blitz with a hand blender until puréed. Add the olive oil and dairy-free milk, weighing them directly in the jug if you like. Then stir in the lemon zest and vanilla.

Mix together the dry ingredients in a large bowl, then make a well in the centre. Pour the wet mixture into the well and gradually whisk in the dry ingredients until only just combined but with no lumps.

Pour the cake batter into the prepared tin. Arrange the pear slices on the top and sprinkle over the extra sugar. Bake for 40–50 minutes until the centre of the cake is firm to the touch.

Leave to cool in the tin for 15 minutes or so before releasing and slicing. Keep in an airtight container for up to 3 days.

INDEX

UK/US GLOSSARY

UK	US	UK	US
Aubergine	Eggplant	Flour, plain	Flour, all-purpose
Baking paper	Parchment paper	Flour, strong white	Flour, white bread
Beans, black-eyed	Peas, black-eyed	Grill	Broil/broiler
Beans, borlotti	Beans, cranberry	Spring onions	Scallions
Beans, butter	Beans, lima	Lentils, Puy	Lentils, French green
Beans, flageolet	Beans, great northern	Mushrooms, chestnut	Mushrooms, cremini
Beans, haricot	Beans, navy	Oats, porridge	Oats, rolled
Beetroot	Beets	Passata	Tomato puree or sauce
Bicarbonate of soda	Baking soda		
Chilli flakes	Dried red pepper flakes	Polenta	Cornmeal
		Pulses, dried	Beans, dried
Clingfilm	Plastic wrap	Spring greens	Collard greens
Coconut, desiccated	Coconut, dry unsweetened	Stock cube	Bouillon cube
		Sugar, caster	Sugar, superfine
Coriander	If referring to the leaves, cilantro	Sugar, icing	Sugar, confectioners'
		Swede	Rutabaga
Cornflour	Cornstarch	Sweetcorn	Corn kernels
Courgette	Zucchini	Tea towel	Dish towel
		Tomato purée	Tomato paste